Where in the World
Published by Orange, a division of The reThink Group, Inc.
5870 Charlotte Lane, Suite 300
Cumming, GA 30040 U.S.A.
The Orange logo is a registered trademark of The reThink Group, Inc.

All Scripture quotations, unless otherwise noted, are taken from the *Holy Bible, New International Version®. NIV®.* Copyright © 1973, 1978, 1984 by International Bible Society. Used by permission of Zondervan.

Other Orange products are available online and direct from the publisher. Visit our website at www.WhatIsOrange.org for more resources like these.

ISBN: 978-1-941259-70-2

©2016 The reThink Group, Inc.

reThink Conceptual Team: Reggie Joiner, Kristen Ivy, Mike Clear, Dan Scott, Jon Williams
Lead Writer: Holly Crawshaw
Lead Editor: Lauren Terrell
Editing Team: Laurin Greco, Mike Jeffries
Art Direction: Ryan Boon
Project Manager: Nate Brandt
Cartooning & Design: Jacob Hunt

Printed in the United States of America
First Edition 2016

1 2 3 4 5 6 7 8 9 10

04/15/16

Copies of this book are available for distribution in churches, schools, and other venues at a significant discount. For more details, go to www.OrangeStore.org

INTRODUCTION

Let's get to know each other. Cool? (Oh, and you're gonna need a pen or pencil for this book.)

WHERE IN THE WORLD . . .
Are you? ....

WHERE IN THE WORLD . . .
Is your favorite restaurant? ....

What do you like to eat there? ....
Mmm . . . now I'm hungry. But don't get up for a snack yet!
We're just getting started . . .

WHERE IN THE WORLD . . .
Would you love to travel one day? ....

(Cool! Can I come?)

WHERE IN THE WORLD . . .
Did you get this book?

....

What do you hope happens when you read it?

....

....

Okay, now let's get a little serious. Don't worry—I don't get serious too often.

WHERE IN THE WORLD . . .

Were you when you first heard the story of Jesus?

What did you think?

Now that I know a little more about you, it's time to introduce myself.

What? You've never had a book introduce itself before? Well, I guess you could say I'm just that awesome.

My name is *Where in the World*. Yeah, you probably already knew that, huh?

My purpose is to help you grow. Not taller, but that might happen, too. I want to help your **faith** grow.

You might think **faith** has something to do with what you *believe*.
You might think **faith** has to do with your relationship with *God*.
You might think **faith** has to do with trusting in something or someone you can't *see*.

And you'd be right. All of those describe the word *faith*. But I'm going to use a different definition. (Again, because I'm just that awesome.)

Faith is believing what Jesus did can change me.

When you believe that Jesus really lived, really died, and was really raised back to life, that *faith* will change your life AND the lives of those around you.

So you're going to get to know Jesus. Like, really get to know Him. Like you know your best friends. You're going to learn . . .

Where in the world Jesus was born.
Where in the world Jesus lived.
Where in the world His friends lived.
Where in the world He died.
And, **where in the world** Jesus went after. *(Hint: it wasn't in this world.)*

But it doesn't stop there.

You're also going to meet a guy named Paul. Just like Jesus, Paul was real. But when the Bible introduces Paul, he's a Jesus-hating Christian hunter.

Dude. Not cool.

But by the end of our time together, you'll see a brand new Paul. How in **the world** did that happen?

I'm going to tell you. But first, here's how I work.

We're going to hang out for *nine weeks*.

For *five* days each week, you'll read *one devotion*.

On the *sixth day*, there's a "Try This" section that you can do or you can skip.

If you miss a day, it's okay. But I don't think you will. After all, the story of Jesus is the greatest story ever told. (Also, did I mention I am *that* awesome?)

Are you ready? Really? Are you sure?! Stretch your arms. Blink your eyes ten times fast. Get comfy wherever you're sitting.

READY, SET . . . TURN THE PAGE!

DAY 1

JESUS' LIFE
THE FOUR GOSPELS

You've heard of Jesus, right? Maybe you've even seen pictures of Him in a book or something. He's usually wearing a long robe that looks like a nightgown and has flowing hair like guys in rock bands.

artist's interpretation

Sometimes it's easy to believe that's all Jesus is—a character in a book who isn't real.

But Jesus is real. Very real.

Jesus was born just like you were born.

Well, maybe not *just* like you were born. When Jesus' mom had Him, she was surrounded by animals. Which may sound awesome, but when you think about the itchy hay, cold wind, and sharing a bed with a goat who smells like old cheese . . . Yeah. Not so much.

The story of Jesus' life is the most epic adventure you'll ever hear. But to tell the *whole* story, I need to rewind . . . and rewind some more.

Rewind to the very beginning. The *beginning of the beginning*. When there was only darkness and nothingness. God had the same thought you're probably having——darkness and nothingness are blah.

So, with His words, God created the world and everything in it in *six* days, resting on the seventh (like a boss).

In the world God created, there was no pain, suffering, or sickness. The first humans—Adam and Eve—were best buds with God. Everything was *perfect*. All Adam and Eve had to do was *not* eat fruit from this one tree.

So guess what Adam and Eve did...

When Adam and Eve broke God's one rule, they sinned and separated themselves from God.

Because God is perfect, He cannot be close to sin.

Adam and Eve's sin broke God's heart along with the perfect world He had created.

God could have decided to put an end to the world and the people He had created. He could've given up. After all, He had only given them one rule and they couldn't even obey it.

But instead of destroying them, God came up with a plan to rescue them: Jesus. That's right. Jesus was a real person who was really sent by God to fix a real problem in the world.

As Jesus grew up, He proved just how special He was.

But not everyone loved Jesus. In fact, some people *hated* Him. These people arrested Jesus. These people *killed* Jesus.

And Jesus *let them*. He could have stopped them at any point, but He didn't. When Jesus gave up His perfect life, He did it because He loves God's creation. He did it because He loves you.

But that's not the best part.

Three days after Jesus was buried, His tomb was empty. *God raised Jesus from the dead.* Over *500* people saw Jesus before He returned to Heaven to live with God.

The story of Jesus is more than a story. It's more than an image of a man in a robe with long hair. It's history—*history* that changed *everything*.

DAY 2

JESUS WAS A CURIOUS KID
LUKE 2:41-52

When you hear the name *Jesus*, what are three words that pop into your mind?

(PS – You'll need a pen or pencil.)
(PPS – Don't worry about spelling. No one's gonna check your work.)

1. The cross - K
2. God   - A
3. Angels - K

Were any of these words on your list?

holy	intelligent	curious
loving	friendly	human
funny	creative	sensitive

Maybe a few, but probably not many. See, it's easy to think of Jesus as a strong and mighty Savior living in Heaven. But when we think about what Jesus was like when He lived on Earth . . .

It's not so easy, is it?

Did you know that Jesus was like you? He was once *your* age. It's kind of weird to think about, right? Did Jesus sleep late? Did He have a favorite food? Was Jesus a fast runner?

If you could ask Jesus one question about His life, what would it be?

K- What is your favorite food?

A- What is your favorite color?

Did you know that the Bible isn't *just* one book? It's actually a bunch of shorter books written by different people. These books were all put together to tell one great story—the story of Jesus. And even though the Bible doesn't tell us *everything* about Jesus' life, it does give us an idea of what He was like growing up.

One of the books of the Bible was written by a guy named Luke. Can you guess what the book Luke wrote was named?

HINT: Luke's name was . . .

That's right! The book Luke wrote was named LUKE. And Luke tells us a very interesting story about Jesus. It's found in *Luke 2:41-52*:

> Every year Jesus' parents went to Jerusalem for the Passover Feast. When Jesus was 12 years old, they went up to the feast as usual. After the feast was over, his parents left to go back home. The boy Jesus stayed behind in Jerusalem.

Hang on. So . . . Jesus didn't follow His parents home?

Nope.

What was Jesus doing that was so important?

Let's get this straight. Jesus stayed behind in Jerusalem . . . to *learn*? Actually, that's exactly what He did. At 12 years old, Jesus wanted to know more about God.

Jesus was a curious kid.

What's something that makes you curious? Put a check beside anything you want to know more about.

❏ **Will your favorite team win their next big game?**
❏ **What are your friends doing this weekend?**
❏ **What will your mom cook for dinner?**
A ☑ **What will happen in the show you love watching?**
K☑ **What grade did you get on your spelling test?**

We're all *curious* about something. Jesus was curious, too. He was especially curious about His heavenly Father—God.

Have you ever thought of Jesus as being a curious kid?

◑ THINK OF ONE OR TWO QUESTIONS ABOUT GOD THAT YOU'RE CURIOUS ABOUT. WRITE THEM HERE.

A - Why does God love me?

Why did God make me?

HERE'S A CHALLENGE FOR YOU: LIKE JESUS DID WITH THE TEACHERS IN OUR STORY, FIND SOMEONE YOU TRUST WHO KNOWS A LOT ABOUT GOD AND ASK THEM YOUR QUESTIONS. COME BACK AND WRITE THEIR RESPONSES HERE.

Because He made you - so you are His daughter. To help others and teach others about Jesus.

DAY 3

JESUS WAS TEMPTED
MATTHEW 4:1-11

What's your favorite dessert ever? Circle your top three from the list below:

 ice cream
apple pie
 cupcakes
candy bar

 brownie
milkshake
cookies
banana pudding

sour candy
tiramisu
cheesecake
fruit salad

Am I missing one? Write it here: popsicles

Okay, be honest. How many of you got up to get a snack after reading that list? (It's okay to raise your hand. I can't see you.)

When you close your eyes and think about your favorite dessert, it's almost like you can taste it. If you hadn't eaten all day long and someone brought you your favorite dessert, you'd probably eat it so fast that it would break some kind of record!

Now, imagine you haven't eaten all day long and someone brings you the most glorious, amazing, incredible dessert ever . . .

. . . but told you all you could do was look at it.

That sounds miserable, right? It would be really hard to ignore that plate of deliciousness because of something called . . . *temptation*.

If you think about it, we have that feeling a lot—the feeling of *wanting* something, but knowing we shouldn't or couldn't have it.

What's the last . . .

- **thing you wanted to buy but couldn't pay for?**

  flipazoo & bike

- **thing you wanted to eat but couldn't eat?**

  candy

- **place you wanted to go that you couldn't go?**

  Mc Donalds

- **app you wanted to download but couldn't download?**

- **thing you wanted to say but couldn't say?**

  Insult - you're stupid

Did you know that **Jesus was tempted**? Seriously. That might be hard for you to believe, because Jesus never sinned. But that doesn't mean Jesus was never *tempted* to sin.

In Matthew 4:1-11, the Bible tells us that Jesus was led into a desert and didn't have anything to eat or drink for 40 days and nights. At that point, we'd all be licking dirt off our sandals for food!

Now, the Bible also tells us that Jesus' number one enemy was in the desert, too. He goes by a few names (the devil, Satan, the evil one), but we'll just call him the enemy. While Jesus was in the desert, the enemy came to Jesus and tempted Him.

If we had been Jesus, we probably would have turned those stones into dodge balls to pelt at the enemy's face. (Right after we turned a couple of them into bread, because let's be honest, Jesus had to be *starving!*)

But Jesus didn't give in to the enemy's temptation. No matter how many times the enemy tried to get Him to do something He shouldn't, Jesus resisted.

Is there anything in your life that you're tempted *to do* or *not to do* that you wish you could resist? Are you tempted to . . .

- **Look at your friend's answers during a math test?**
- **Lie to your parents about having homework?**
- **Stay up too late watching TV or YouTube videos?**
- **Eat snacks when you're not supposed to?**
- **Play video games when you should be studying?**

Just like you and everyone else on Earth, **Jesus was tempted**. But unlike you and everyone else on Earth, Jesus *never* gave in to temptation.

Open up your Bible or Bible App and read the ways the enemy tempted Jesus in Matthew 4:1-11.

◑ BELOW, WRITE A PRAYER ASKING GOD TO HELP YOU RESIST SOME OF YOUR BIGGEST TEMPTATIONS.

Dear God - please give me strength not to do bad things I know I shouldn't, like get up when it's bed time.

DAY 4

JESUS WAS A FRIEND
JOHN 11:1-44

In the box below, write down your best friend's name and sketch his or her portrait. (If you have more than one best friend, squeeze them all in!)

What's one of your favorite memories with that friend?

- **Maybe you saw a really funny movie together.**
- **Maybe you had a sleepover with them where you stayed up super late.**
- **Maybe you watched your favorite sports team win the big game together.**

Draw a quick sketch that represents that memory.

Watched Little Rascals

Played outside

What about some not-so-awesome memories?

- **Has your friend ever hurt your feelings?**
- **Have you ever gotten into a fight with them?**
- **Have they ever done something that annoyed you?**

All friendships have good times and hard times, too.

When Jesus was on Earth, He hung out a *lot* with other people. But did you know Jesus wasn't just a leader and a teacher? Did you know that **Jesus was a friend**? What mattered to Jesus' friends, mattered to Jesus. They had good times, and they had hard times, too.

We can read about one of those hard times in John 11:7-44.

Jesus was friends with two sisters named Mary and Martha. Mary and Martha had a brother named Lazarus who was Jesus' good friend, too. And Lazarus? Well, Lazarus got sick and died.

The Bible says that Jesus came to visit the sisters after Lazarus died. And when Jesus saw how sad everyone was, it bothered Him.

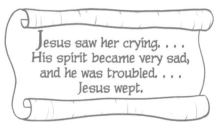

Jesus saw her crying. . . .
His spirit became very sad,
and he was troubled. . . .
Jesus wept.

John 11:33, 35

Jesus was more than a leader and a teacher. **Jesus was a friend**. And just like He got sad when Mary and Martha got sad, He gets sad when you get sad, too.

Pretend that Jesus is sitting beside you. Spend a few minutes telling Him what makes you sad. It can be out loud, whispered, in your head, or written out. He will hear you. He cares.

⊙ EXTRA CREDIT: GRAB YOUR BIBLE AND READ THE ENTIRE STORY OF WHAT HAPPENED WITH LAZARUS IN JOHN 11:1-44. *(SPOILER: JESUS DID SOMETHING SO AMAZING THAT YOUR MIND IS GONNA BE BLOWN!)*

K- when people take things away from me (throw hat out window)

DAY 5

JESUS WAS OBEDIENT
MATTHEW 26:36-46

Today's story takes place in a garden. Draw a quick sketch of what a *garden* looks like.

For a lot of us, when we think about a garden, we think about flowers blooming, vegetables growing, and birds singing. We think about sunshine and blue skies. Gardens are a happy place.

But that's not true for the garden we're going to talk about.

In Matthew 26:36-46, we read about a garden called Gethsemane. Yeah, that's kind of a weird word. It sounds like this: *Geth/sim/uh/nee*. (Try saying that five times fast!) And it wasn't full of flowers or rows of veggies—this garden was full of olive trees.

Jesus and some of His friends went to this garden the night Jesus was arrested.

Did you know that Jesus was *arrested*? He was. He was arrested by people who didn't believe He was God's Son.

But here's the unbelievable part—Jesus knew He was going to be arrested. He also knew that after His arrest, He would be killed.

Whoa. That's heavy, right?

Right! And that's why Jesus went to the garden. Thinking about everything that was about to happen made His heart feel heavy. He looked at His friends and said, *"My soul is very sad" (Matthew 26:38)*. The Bible says that Jesus fell to the ground, put His face down in the dirt and began to pray.

If you had been Jesus, what would you have prayed?

God Pretect me, from this battle.

Ready for this? Jesus prayed:

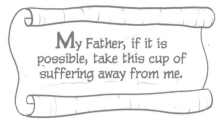

My Father, if it is possible, take this cup of suffering away from me.

Matthew 26:39

In other words, "Hey, so, God? About this whole getting arrested and dying thing . . . I really don't want to do it."

Was that close to your answer? Are you surprised? Check out what Jesus said next:

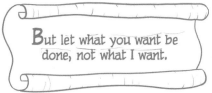

But let what you want be done, not what I want.

Matthew 26:39

You know what happened next? Jesus was arrested. Jesus was killed. He could have run away. He could have performed a miracle that kept Him safe. But instead, **Jesus obeyed**.

Jesus obeyed because He knew that by dying He was doing what God had sent Him to do. And three days later, God raised Jesus back to life!

❷ GO BACK TO YOUR SKETCH OF THE GARDEN. FIND A SPACE TO WRITE DOWN THREE WAYS YOU CAN OBEY. SPEND A FEW MINUTES ASKING GOD TO HELP YOU OBEY, JUST LIKE HE HELPED JESUS.

TRY THIS

Remember on Day 1 when we talked about Adam and Eve? When Adam and Eve disobeyed God, they *sinned*.

What does it mean *to sin*?

to not oBey GOd

Here's the thing . . . and this is never fun to talk about . . . *you sin, too.* Everyone sins. Everyone, that is, except Jesus.

So when Jesus gave up His *perfect* life, He paid the price for *everyone's* sin. Including yours.

Take a minute and think about some of the times you've messed up. A lie you told your mom . . . that time you disobeyed your dad . . . something mean you said to your little brother or sister . . . when you didn't keep your friend's secret . . . when you left someone out on purpose.

Write a few examples here: (Don't worry—nobody's going to read this!)

not listening to mommy

The Bible says when we tell Jesus that we believe He's God's Son, we get total forgiveness for all of our sins. In exchange for our faith, we get a brand new start.

Now go back and mark through each and every one of the examples you wrote. Scribble them out until you can't even see them anymore. Because if you've invited Jesus to live in your heart, each one is totally forgiven. Erased. Gone.

(If you want to thank Jesus for completely erasing sin from your life, feel free!)

Maybe you've already started a relationship with Jesus. Maybe you haven't. Maybe you aren't really sure what that even means. Look at the line below. You are on one side and Jesus is on the other side. Draw a star on the line that shows how close you feel to Jesus right now.

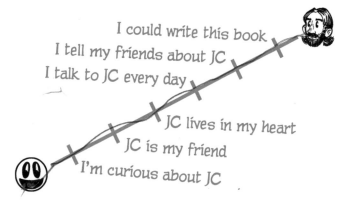

I could write this book
I tell my friends about JC
I talk to JC every day
JC lives in my heart
JC is my friend
I'm curious about JC

Your star may not be very far up the line. That's okay! That's why you're reading this book—so your faith can grow bigger and bigger as you get to know the story of Jesus better and better.

➲ AS YOU CONTINUE READING THIS JOURNAL, COME BACK TO THIS PAGE AT THE END OF EACH WEEK AND DRAW A NEW STAR.

DAY 1

PAUL
ACTS 7:34-60 • ACTS 9:1-25

Saul was one of the scariest dudes in the Bible. He traveled from city to city arresting people who loved Jesus. If punishing Jesus-followers were a sport, Saul would have been voted Most Valuable Player.

Paul loved Jesus more than life itself. He traveled from city to city spreading the news about Jesus and His love. If following Jesus were a sport, Paul would have been voted Most Valuable Player.

Now, prepare your minds to be blown . . .

Saul and Paul were the same person.

Yeah. Saul went by Saul and he also went by Paul. And he has an *amazing* story.

When Paul was younger, Paul didn't believe that Jesus was God's Son. And when people disagreed with Paul, it made him mad.

- Madder than your mom when you got permanent marker on the sofa.
- Madder than your dad when you slammed your bike into his car.
- Madder than your teacher when your class acts like wild gorillas who escaped from the zoo.

So Paul started hunting Jesus-followers and throwing them in prison.

But, wait. If Paul was a Christian-hater, how did he become one of the greatest Christians who ever lived?

Glad you asked.

Paul and some other men were traveling to a town called Damascus to arrest more Jesus-followers. Without warning, a light brighter than the sun flashed from the sky and a voice thundered down.

Paul's men led him into Damascus where he stayed *blind* for three days. That's right. Paul couldn't see a thing.

In Damascus, a Jesus-follower (the kind of guy Paul used to arrest) named Ananias heard Jesus speak to *him*.

Ananias was really afraid (you know, because of the whole Paul's-a-Christian-hater thing), but he obeyed. When Ananias found Paul, he put his hands on Paul and prayed for him.

Paul's sight returned. He regained his strength. But most importantly, he *knew* that Jesus is God's Son.

After Paul met Jesus, *everything* changed. He was brand new. He was more like the Paul we've come to know and love—Paul, the MVP of following Jesus.

Out of everyone Jesus could have chosen to be His MVP, He chose Paul—a guy who had done a lot of terrible things.

It's easy for us to see ourselves as someone Jesus wouldn't or couldn't use. Maybe we don't feel smart enough, brave enough, or good enough. But when Paul met Jesus, it changed *everything*. And we know that **the story of Jesus has the power to change everything for you, too.**

DAY 2

PAUL'S PRIORITIES
ACTS 9:1-9

When you're awake, your brain produces enough energy to power a light bulb.[1] (Think of all the money you could be saving your parents!)

Your mind is constantly juggling different thoughts. You think about . . .

grades	tv shows
friends	shopping
video games	playing outside
sports	family
God	music

In the space on the next page → → → rewrite that list of words. Only, put the items in order of what's *most important* to you. Your #1 should be the #1 most important thing in your life.

Helpful Hint: Don't answer how you *think* you should answer. Answer by asking yourself some questions . . .

- **What is the first thing I do when I get home from school?**
- **What do I want most when I get time alone to myself?**
- **If I could only think about one thing for the next hour, what would it be?**

Whatever your answers are, those are things you should put near the top of your list. Ready? And . . . GO!

1

2.

3.

4.

5.

6.

7.

8.

9.

10.

Whatever your #1 answer is, that's the main *priority* in your life. Priority is a word that means *what's important to you.*

Circle any sentence below that's true for you:
- That was hard because I don't really care about any of those things.
- That was hard because there are a lot of things that are really important to me.
- I'm surprised by my #1 answer.
- I'm surprised by my #10 answer.
- I'm not surprised about anything.
- I hate surprises.

Our priorities act like a steering wheel. Imagine that your life is a car. A cool car. A more-than-cool car. Like a jacked-up SUV or a super-fast racecar. In the space below, draw a quick sketch of what your life's car would look like.

Now, draw a steering wheel in your car. (If you already drew one, pat yourself on the back!)

In your life, the things that are most important to you move you. Just like a steering wheel in a car controls the way the car turns, your priorities control whether you'll watch TV, get on your tablet, or do your homework.

Think about Paul's life. Before he met Jesus, his priority list probably looked like this:

1. Stop the Jesus-followers
2. Encourage others to stop the Jesus-followers
3. Eat flatbread

But after Jesus spoke to Paul, Paul's entire life changed. Including his priorities. His new list was very short:

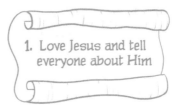

1. Love Jesus and tell everyone about Him

What was important to Paul changed. And that single priority steered his life in a completely new direction. That's because **the story of Jesus changes what's important**.

Take a look at your list again. Are your priorities steering you in the right direction? Are you . . .

Praying daily?
Reading your Bible regularly?
Practicing the instrument you begged your parents for?
Turning in your homework on time?
Using your talents to help others?

❯ IN THE SPACE BELOW, WRITE DOWN SOMETHING YOU CAN DO *TOMORROW* TO IMPROVE YOUR LIST OF PRIORITIES.

....

....

....

....

DAY 3

ANANIAS
ACTS 9:10-19

Do you know what the word *phobia* means? Phobias are extreme fears. And people have some pretty strange phobias. Like . . .

Aulophobia is the fear of *flutes.*
Genuphobia is the fear of *knees.*
Arithmophobia is the fear of *numbers.*
Peladophobia is the fear of *bald people.*
Omphalphobia is the fear of *belly buttons.*

Okay. That last one actually makes sense. Belly buttons *are* kinda weird-looking.

For you, maybe it's the dark. Or speaking in front of a lot of people. Or clowns. Or those dolls whose eyes open and shut. We all have fears. We all have things that make us nervous or afraid.

What are some of your fears? Write a few of them below:

....

....

....

When we read about Paul's life, we meet another guy named Ananias. And Ananias had one very specific fear . . . *PAUL.*

So when God spoke to Ananias and told him to go pray for Paul, Ananias didn't want to do it. He said:

Lord . . . I've heard many reports about this man. They say he has done great harm.

Acts 9:13

In other words, "Um . . . Lord? You know that dude's gonna arrest me for following You, right?"

But the Bible says that God told Ananias to pray with Paul. So guess what Ananias did?

Because when you know the story of Jesus, **it makes you brave**. And here's a little secret about being brave . . .

(You have to read the next sentence in a whisper.)

Being brave doesn't mean your fear goes away.

Nope. Being brave simply means believing that God is always with you.

◑ IN THE SPACES BELOW, FILL IN THE BLANKS WITH YOUR FEARS. READ THE SENTENCES OUT LOUD. READ THEM EVERY DAY IF YOU HAVE TO!

When I am afraid of .... ,
God is with me.

When I am afraid of .... ,
God is with me.

When I am afraid of .... ,
God is with me.

WHEN YOU'RE FINISHED, PRAY AND ASK GOD TO MAKE YOU BRAVE. ASK HIM TO REMIND YOU THAT WHEN YOU'RE AFRAID, HE IS ALWAYS WITH YOU. JUST LIKE HE WAS ALWAYS WITH PAUL. JUST LIKE HE WAS ALWAYS WITH ANANIAS.

DAY 4

PAUL PREACHES
ACTS 9:20-21

What's your favorite . . .

Food?

....

TV show?

....

Sports team?

....

App/video game?

....

Song?

....

If I were to ask your friends and family what your favorites are, they'd probably know at least some of those answers, right?

Whether it's a new album, the latest book in a series, or the best player on your favorite team, when you love something, you talk about it.

When Paul met Jesus while traveling down the road to Damascus, he realized that he had been wrong. Paul realized that Jesus *is* God's Son. The Bible says that as soon as Paul was able, he did one thing:

Right away he began to preach in the synagogues. He taught that Jesus is the Son of God.

Acts 9:20

Paul didn't care that he was going to make all his old friends angry. Paul didn't care that people were going to whisper about him behind his back. Paul had just learned the story of Jesus, and that made him want to tell others about Him.

Just like Paul, **the story of Jesus makes us want to tell others about Him, too**.

But before you get started, it's important to think about what you're going to say and how you're going to say it.

THE WHAT

Write down three words or phrases that you would use to describe Jesus:

Example: Obedient to God

....

....

....

Now, write down three things you know about the story of Jesus (Look at Week 1, Day 1 if you need help remembering):

Example: God sent us Jesus as a baby born in Bethlehem.

....

....

....

THE HOW

Now that you know what you're going to say, you can look for ways to bring up the story of Jesus with your friends. The next time you're on the bus, the playground, soccer practice, or just hanging at your neighbor's house, you could start by saying something like . . .

"I'm reading a new book called *Where in the World*. The coolest thing I've learned so far is . . ."

(You might want to mention that I am the funniest, greatest, bestest devotional journal of all time!)

Think of one friend you'd like to share the story of Jesus with. Write down his or her name in the box below.

> **◐ SPEND A MINUTE PRAYING THAT GOD WOULD HELP YOU TELL THIS PERSON THE STORY OF JESUS.**

DAY 5

PAUL ESCAPES
ACTS 9:19B-25

Write down the names of your closest friends.

....

....

....

....

....

Out of all those friends, who would you go to first if you needed help? Circle his or her name.

Whoever you circled must be someone you *trust*. When you *trust* someone, you depend on them. You need them. You feel safe asking them to be there for you.

Before Paul became a Jesus-follower, he probably had lots of friends. He went to school with boys his age who believed the same things he did. He worked with a bunch of guys who believed the same things he did. He went to the Jewish temple with a bunch of people who believed the same things he did.

We tend to trust people who believe the same things we do.

So what happened when Paul started believing something different? The Bible says he spent several days hanging out with people who followed Jesus, too. Check out **Acts 9:23-25**.

After many days, the Jews had a meeting. They planned to kill Paul. But he learned about their plan. Day and night they watched the city gates closely in order to kill him. But his followers helped him escape by night. They lowered him in a basket through an opening in the wall.

The story of Jesus changed who Paul trusted—in a *big* way.

The people Paul *used* to trust decided to *kill* him. But because Paul had surrounded himself with new friends he trusted, he was able to escape Damascus with their help.

The story of Jesus changes who we trust, too.

It's okay to have friends who believe differently than you do. In fact, that's a good thing!

But when it comes to who you trust to . . .

. . . answer questions about your faith,

. . . give great advice,

. . . or pray with you for clear answers,

trust people who believe the same things you do—people who know the story of Jesus.

Think about your group of friends. Is there someone close to you who knows the story of Jesus? Is there someone close to you who wants to know the story of Jesus better?

Make this the person you trust.

When you need them, they'll be able to pray with you. They'll be able to tell you what the Bible says you should do. They'll also need you to do the same for them, which will help you grow in your faith.

And, hey, if you ever need to get out of town by being lowered in a basket, you'll know exactly who to call.

TRY THIS

The story of Jesus changes . . .

. . . our priorities.

. . . our fears.

. . . our friends

. . . and how we share His message.

The story of Jesus changes everything.

Think back on days 2-5 of this week. Which of these changes will be the most challenging for you?

....

....

Why?

....

....

....

When we do hard things, it stretches our faith. It makes us grow, and it makes us stronger.

TAKE A WALK OUTSIDE TODAY AND FIND A ROCK. BRING THAT ROCK INSIDE (MAYBE WASH IT OFF A LITTLE BIT) AND WRITE THE WORD "FAITH" ON IT. PUT THE ROCK SOMEWHERE YOU'LL SEE IT EVERY DAY.

LET THIS ROCK REMIND YOU THAT WITH GOD'S HELP, YOU CAN DO HARD THINGS.

DAY I

BARNABAS
ACTS 9:26-31

Last week you learned about a guy named Paul. Do you remember Paul's other name?

Saul.

Good! You've been paying attention.

After Jesus spoke to Paul on the road to Damascus, Paul's life got flipped upside down. Paul went from being the man who arrested Jesus-followers to being a Jesus-follower himself!

But that's not the end of Paul's story. In fact, it's just the beginning.

Think about your best friend. What if you didn't see your friend for a few weeks, and the next time you hung out, they were like a totally different person? The way they talked was different. Their attitude was different. Even their beliefs were different!

You'd be confused, right? You might even think they were faking it. And that's exactly what happened to Paul when he went to meet with the Jesus-followers at Jesus-Follower Headquarters (a.k.a. Jerusalem).

Finally, Paul raised his fist and knocked. What do you think Jesus' friends did?

But there was one Jesus-follower named Barnabas who was brave enough to listen to Paul. And then brave enough to tell the other Jesus-followers how Paul had really changed . . .

. . . how Paul had met Jesus on the road to Damascus.
. . . how Paul had become a true follower of Jesus.

The Bible says that after Barnabas stood up for Paul, the other Jesus-followers welcomed him. And Paul immediately started traveling around Jerusalem, telling everyone that Jesus is God's Son.

Eventually, Paul started many of the first churches, leading countless people to put their faith in Jesus.

What would have happened if Barnabas hadn't stood up for Paul? Thankfully, we never had to find out.

Barnabas gave Paul a chance because he knew Jesus could change a man as cruel and ruthless as Paul. And the same is true for you. **When you know the story of Jesus, it changes how you see others.**

DAY 2

PAUL'S FRIENDS
ACTS 9:26

What are some of your favorite things to do with your friends?

sports	going to the playground
creating art	eating junk food
watching movies	video games
listening to music	science experiments
playing music	taking pictures
card games	making videos
visiting the park	bowling

Are there any missing? Choose one (or make up your own) and draw a quick picture of you and your friends doing that activity together.

There's something you should know. And it's kind of a bummer . . .

You may keep one or two close friends your entire life, but for the most part, who you're friends with is going to change.

Write down the name of a friend and tell us how you met.

When Paul decided to follow Jesus, he joined up with other believers in Damascus. But when he had to leave Damascus, he had to leave those friendships behind.

So what did Paul do?

The Bible tells us in Acts 9:26 that when Paul went to Jerusalem, he tried to join the Jesus-followers there. Some of those believers had been Jesus' *best friends*—they were called the Disciples. They had spent a lot of time with Jesus, and they loved Him. Paul wanted to know more about Jesus, so he hung out with the people who knew Him best.

Paul realized, and maybe you're realizing too, that **the story of Jesus changes who we want to hang out with**.

Just like Paul, it's important for you to choose your friends.

Not just because you sit on the bus together.

Not just because your moms are friends.

Not just because someone is funny.

It's important to give your time to people who also know and love Jesus.

◑ WRITE DOWN THE NAMES OF THREE PEOPLE AROUND YOUR AGE WHO KNOW AND LOVE JESUS. MAYBE THIS IS SOMEONE IN YOUR SMALL GROUP. MAYBE IT'S A COUSIN OR NEIGHBOR. OR MAYBE IT'S SOMEONE YOU KNOW FROM SCHOOL.

1.

....

2.

....

3.

....

LOOK BACK AT YOUR FAVORITE THING TO DO WITH FRIENDS. WITH YOUR PARENTS' PERMISSION, PLAN TO HANG OUT WITH SOMEBODY ON YOUR LIST BY DOING ONE OF YOUR FAVORITE ACTIVITIES TOGETHER.

DAY 3

BARNABAS FINDS PAUL
ACTS 9:26-31

Grab a pen and find a mirror. (Don't forget to bring this book!)

Maybe there's a mirror in your bedroom hanging over your dresser. Maybe you have a mirror in your hallway or bathroom.

Now, study your face in the mirror. Without writing their actual color, **how would you describe your eyes?**

....

....

How about the shape of your face?

....

....

Now smile. What does your nose do?

....

....

How many teeth can you see?

....

Chances are, no one else reading this book wrote the same answers as you. That's because God created each of us to be different.

When Paul visited the Jesus-followers in Jerusalem, the Bible says they were afraid of him. Acts 9:26 says the believers didn't think Paul had really changed. They thought he was still the Jesus-hating dude who threw people like them in jail.

But if you read on, Acts 9:27-31 says Barnabas (remember him from a couple days ago?) was willing to give Paul a chance.

Have you ever felt nervous about being friends with someone who is different from you? Or worried some of your other friends would make fun of you?

It's easy to show kindness to people you know—to people who are like you. But when you follow Jesus, your faith should help you show the same kindness to everyone. Even to people who are different from you.

Jesus changes how we see people who are different from us.

Instead of seeing someone who is different from you, you'll start to see someone you can show Jesus' love to.

That's exactly what Barnabas did when he brought Paul to the other Jesus-followers.

Now, you probably won't travel to Jerusalem to find a guy who is scared for his life and make him feel better like Barnabas did, but you can . . .

Share your tablet.
Ask someone to sit beside you at lunch.
Give away the apple you're not going to eat.
Hold the door open.
Give a fist bump.

❷ ON THE NEXT PAGE, THERE'S A HUGE LETTER B. TRACE IT ONTO ANOTHER SHEET OF PAPER AND TAPE IT UP SOMEWHERE IN YOUR ROOM. EVERY TIME YOU SEE IT, REMEMBER TO . . .

BE LIKE BARNABAS

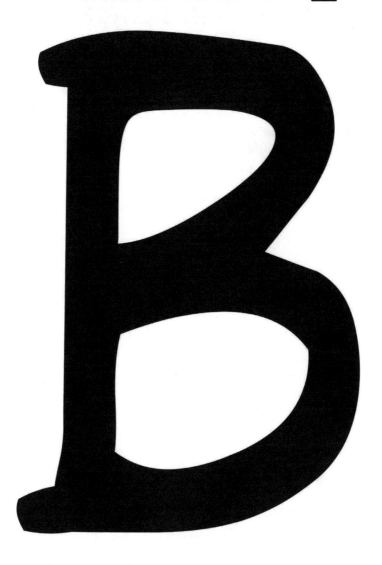

DAY 4

PAUL'S CHALLENGE
ACTS 9:28-30

When's the last time you were scared or afraid? Was it:
> . . . during a thunderstorm?
> . . . when you almost fell off your skateboard?
> . . . at your piano recital?
> . . . after you dropped your mom's phone facedown on the pavement?

....

....

Have you ever paid attention to what happens to your body when you're afraid? Write down what you think happens to your. . .

Hands:

....

Head:

....

Heart:

....

Our bodies react to fear in very similar ways. Sweaty. Shaky. Heart pounding. Being afraid is no fun for anyone.

We already know when Paul first started following Jesus in Damascus, he began telling others about Jesus right away. That made Paul's old friends really mad. *So mad that they decided to kill Paul.* But Paul escaped Damascus and joined the Jesus-followers in Jerusalem.

Until . . .

The Bible says that after Paul began living with the believers, he:

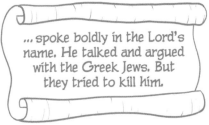

... spoke boldly in the Lord's name. He talked and argued with the Greek Jews. But they tried to kill him.

Acts 9:28-29

Seriously?!?!

It seems like everywhere Paul went, people tried to kill him for preaching about Jesus! What would you have done if you were Paul?

    A.   **Pretend I didn't follow Jesus anymore.**
    B.   **Hire a really scary-looking bodyguard.**
    C.   **Change my name.**
    D.   **Wear a disguise.**
    E.   **Move far, far away.**
    F.   **All of the above.**
    G.   **Keep preaching.**

Paul went with option G because he didn't see losing his life as the challenge. Instead, he saw people needing to hear the story of Jesus as the challenge. Jesus changed how Paul saw challenges.

Sometimes, it's easy to see small things as big challenges. Like:

    . . . **wanting your own phone**
    . . . **not going to the beach for Spring Break**
    . . . **not making the team or squad**
    . . . **completing your chores**
    . . . **arguing with friends**

While these may feel challenging, we learn from Paul that they're not the most important challenge.

We live in a world that needs to hear about Jesus and His love. *That* is our most important challenge. **Jesus changes how we see challenges.**

⟳ LIST THREE WAYS YOU CAN CHALLENGE YOURSELF TO SHOW JESUS' LOVE TO PEOPLE, THEN FOCUS ON THOSE CHALLENGES INSTEAD!

Examples:
1. *I will teach my little brother how to play that game he's been asking about.*
2. *I will not talk back to my mom when she asks me to help with chores.*
3. *I will pick out three toys by the end of this week to donate.*

NOW IT'S YOUR TURN!

1.
....

....
2.
....

....
3.
....

....

DAY 5

GOD CHOSE PAUL
1 TIMOTHY 1:12-18

Grab some markers or colored pencils. (I'll wait for you right here.) Got 'em? Good. In the frame below, draw a self-portrait.

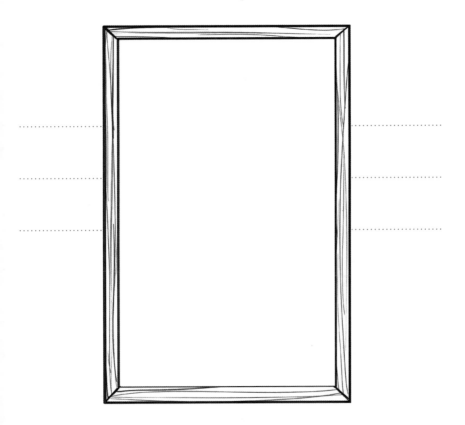

What are three things you really like about yourself? Do you slay at Minecraft? Did you get all A's last year? Are you the fastest kid on your lacrosse team? Write those things on the left side of your self-portrait.

On the other side, write three things you don't really like about yourself. Do you wish you were better at math? Are you bummed that your two front teeth are *still* missing? Would you like to be taller like your brother?

We all *see* ourselves in a unique way. We have opinions about ourselves. We like things about ourselves, and we don't like things about ourselves.

Before Paul was a Jesus-follower, he was a . . . wait a minute. You should know this by now. You tell *us*. Before Paul was a Jesus-follower, he . . .

....

....

....

Grab your Bible or turn on your Bible App. Look up 1 Timothy 1:12-18. Timothy is one of the books of the Bible Paul wrote himself. So keep that in mind as you read.

Done? Great!

Out of all the people in the world, Jesus chose *Paul* to be one of the most important Christians of all time. He says so in verse 16:

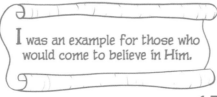

I was an example for those who would come to believe in Him.

1 Timothy 1:16

Knowing the story of Jesus changed how Paul saw himself.

Did you know that Jesus wants to use you just like He used Paul? It doesn't matter:

. . . **how young you are.**
. . . **if your parents are still married to each other.**
. . . **how long you've had a relationship with Jesus.**
. . . **how much money your family has.**
. . . **how many times you've messed up.**

Remember those things you listed about yourself that you don't like? They don't matter, either. Just like all the terrible things Paul had done didn't matter after he met Jesus.

Jesus wants to use you. No matter what. **So let the story of Jesus change how you see yourself.**

❂ GO BACK TO THE THREE THINGS YOU WROTE ON THE RIGHT SIDE OF YOUR SELF-PORTRAIT. CROSS EACH ONE OUT AND WRITE (WHEREVER YOU CAN FIT IT IN): "I CAN BE AN EXAMPLE AND SHOW OTHERS GOD'S LOVE."

TRY THIS

Barnabas will always be remembered as the one Jesus-follower who stuck up for Paul.

One of the few things that all people have in common is that one day, our lives as we know them will stop. That's kinda weird to think about, but it's true.

And just like we talk about Barnabas, someone is going to talk about the kind of person you were.

When you know the story of Jesus, it changes how you see others. It changes how you:

. . . talk to your mom when she's annoying you.
. . . treat your sister when she asks to borrow your stuff.
. . . see the kid sitting alone on the playground.
. . . respect adults.
. . . serve your friends.

The main thing we think about when someone is gone is *how they treated others.*

◑ TAKE A FEW MINUTES TO WALK AROUND YOUR HOUSE. AS YOU DO, WRITE DOWN WORDS THAT DESCRIBE WHAT YOU SEE.

Pictures of your family

Your room (Maybe now is a good time to put those dirty socks in the hamper.)

....

Your book bag

....

Look in the mirror

....

DID YOU SEE ANYTHING THAT SHOWS HOW YOU'RE SEEING OTHERS DIFFERENTLY? IF NOT, WHAT'S ONE THING YOU COULD DO THIS WEEK TO MAKE SURE YOU'RE TREATING OTHERS WELL?

....

DAY 1

PAUL IN ANTIOCH
ACTS 11:25-30 • 13:1-3

Let's be honest—sometimes it's hard to believe some of the things we read in the Bible. Take Paul's story, for example.

But part of having faith is knowing that it's *Jesus* who makes the unbelievable . . . *believable*.

So when you read the rest of Paul's story, keep in mind that no matter how unbelievable things get, *he was a real dude*.

We left off last week with Paul joining the believers in Jerusalem (thanks to Barnabas, winner of the Friend-of-the-Millennium award).

Becoming a Jesus-follower put Paul's life in danger. Seriously. Even his old friends felt so betrayed by Paul's new faith that they made plans to kill him. More than once! But the danger never stopped Paul from telling everyone he could that Jesus *is* God's Son.

Okay, let's fast forward a little bit. More and more people were believing that Jesus is God's Son. More and more people were gathering together to talk about Jesus. And before long, the number of people following Jesus grew from a few to . . .

After a while, Barnabas and Paul met back up in a town called Antioch where the number of Jesus-followers was growing crazy fast. One day, a prophet named Agabus visited them at the church there.

First of all, *Agabus*? Let's hope he had a second name like our bud Saul/Paul.

And second of all, a prophet? Well, a prophet was someone who was so tight with God that God told them what was going to happen before it actually happened. Which sounds kind of awesome, unless your parents are prophets and you have plans to skip your homework. That would be the opposite of awesome.

So, while Agabus was at the church in Antioch, he told them about a prophecy God had shown him. He told them that a huge famine was coming, and that it would spread across the entire world. A famine is when crops don't grow and people can't get enough food to eat. Famines are a really, really scary thing—especially back then.

So the new believers in Antioch decided to do something really cool.

Big deal, you might think. *I shared a PB&J with my little sister yesterday.*

But this was a *huge* deal.

The people in Antioch had *just* started to believe that Jesus is God's Son. For them to send what little food they had to people they'd never met was a *big* sign of their *big* faith in Jesus. And their faith was big because they knew something important: Jesus would give them exactly what they needed. They saw how Jesus took care of them, and it made them want to take care of others.

The same should be true for us . . . **The story of Jesus changes how we help others.**

DAY 2

CHEERFUL GIVER
2 CORINTHIANS 9:7

Grab a pen and this book and take a walk around your house. If you're doing this before bedtime and you're supposed to be in bed, tell your parents they can thank us later.

(Seriously, parents. Let your kid out of their room for just a few minutes. It'll be worth it.)

In each room you walk into, draw a check beside any of the following that you see:

- ❑ **Dishes in the sink**
- ❑ **Unmade bed**
- ❑ **Dirty laundry on the floor**
- ❑ **Full trashcans**
- ❑ **Smudged windows**
- ❑ **Empty drink containers**
- ❑ **Dirty rugs or carpets**
- ❑ **Dusty furniture**
- ❑ **Hungry or restless pets**
- ❑ **Toys scattered on the floor**

Your parents are busy.

You've probably heard them say that. But it's true. Taking care of kids is awesome, but it's a ton of work. And sometimes, your parents need your help.

One of the best ways you can help others is by serving your family at home. And I'm not just talking about your regular chores. I'm talking about helping without being asked.

I know! It's crazy, right? Doing *work* without being asked? Why would anyone do that?

For starters, the Bible tells us to.

We've been talking a lot about Paul. After Paul started following Jesus, he helped many groups of believers start the very first churches in history. He wrote letters to many of these churches, giving them advice and encouraging them.

One letter is a book in the Bible called 2 Corinthians. In it, Paul says this:

> Each of you should give what you have decided in your heart to give. You shouldn't give if you don't want to. You shouldn't give because you are forced to. God loves a cheerful giver.

2 Corinthians 9:7

Paul tells the church that they shouldn't give because they *have* to, but they should give because they *want* to. And when they give, they shouldn't mumble and complain while they do it, because God loves a *cheerful* giver.

In the same way, when you serve your family without being asked—when you clean up a mess you didn't even make, God *loves* that. You're giving one of the most valuable things you have to give: a helping hand!

Look back at the checklist on page 84. Mark out anything that's already your chore. Now, choose *one* helpful task and get it done! But remember . . . put a smile on your face while you do it.

Actually, let's all practice our smiles right now. On three, everybody say, *cheeeeese!*

One.
Two.
Three.

Good! Now, complete your one task and go back to wherever you were when you started today's journal. Don't worry, I'll wait.

❂ DON'T FORGET THAT YOU CAN *LOOK FOR WAYS TO HELP OTHERS* EVERYWHERE YOU GO. AT SCHOOL, A FRIEND'S HOUSE, THE GROCERY STORE, OR CHURCH. BECAUSE WHEN YOU GIVE AND SERVE CHEERFULLY WITHOUT BEING ASKED, YOU'RE BEING JUST LIKE JESUS.

DAY 3

CHURCH ANTIOCH
ACTS 11:25-30

What did you get for Christmas last year? How about the year before that? What about your last few birthdays? Take a few seconds to write down as many gifts as you can remember.

....

....

....

....

....

Now, circle any that you haven't played with or used in the last month. How many circles do you have?

....

Chances are, you can't even remember all the presents you received over the years. But if you looked under your bed, in the back corner of your closet, or in the bottom of the toy box, you'd find stuff you didn't even know you still had.

The church in Antioch—you read about them on Day 1 of this week—didn't have a ton of stuff to give, but they gave anyway. And they didn't just give a little. The Bible says:

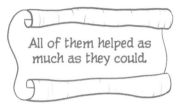

All of them helped as
much as they could.

Acts 11:25:29

Most of us have way more *stuff* than we actually need. I'm not
here to make you feel bad about that, but I do want to help
you figure out how to do something helpful with all your extra
stuff.

You can . . .

...donate
toys I don't play
with!

Or . . .

- Let a classmate use your tablet during technology time.
- Split your lunch with a kid who forgot theirs.
- Drop off clothes and shoes you don't wear anymore to a thrift store.
- Ask your birthday party guests to bring an unwrapped gift to take to a children's hospital.

You can **help others with your stuff** just like the believers in Antioch did.

Go find your mom or dad.

WARNING:
If they're sleeping or taking a shower,
wait until they're finished!

◐ SHOW YOUR MOM OR DAD THE LIST YOU JUST READ. ASK THEM HOW YOU CAN START HELPING OTHERS WITH YOUR STUFF THIS WEEK. THEN, MAKE A PLAN.

HELP OTHERS WITH MY STUFF MASTER PLAN:

What you're gonna do: ....
....
....

How you're gonna do it: ....
....
....

When you're gonna do it by: ....
....
....

After you've made your plan, *you're in charge*. Let your mom or dad look through whatever you decide to give away, but make sure *you're* the person who does all the work.

And you don't have to stop there. You can ask your friends, neighbors, even your church to pitch in.

❷ BEFORE YOU CLOSE THIS BOOK, SPEND A FEW MOMENTS PRAYING. THANK GOD FOR ALL THE STUFF HE HAS GIVEN YOU. ASK HIM TO HELP YOU BE LIKE THE CHURCH IN ANTIOCH BY *HELPING OTHERS WITH YOUR STUFF.*

DAY 4

DO GOOD
HEBREWS 13:16

Check out these cool facts about time[1]:

- **On Mercury, a day (sunrise to sunrise) is *two years* long.**
- **There actually *aren't* 24 hours in one day. Technically, there are 23 hours, 56 minutes, and 4.2 seconds.**
- **Because light takes time to reach us, everything we see is actually *in the past*. If the sun is shining where you are, go check it out. You're seeing what that sun looked like 8 minutes and 20 seconds ago!**

You probably don't think about time much right now. You know when you wake up, when you go to bed, what time school starts and ends, and of course, what time lunch starts.

But as you get older, you'll see how *important* time is. Look at your clock right now. Write down the exact date and time you see.

Today's Date:

....

The Time Right Now:

....

Here's the thing: the moment you just wrote down? You'll *never* get to have that moment again. There's only one moment like that in the history of the world. You know what that means? Your time is valuable.

Knowing that, you shouldn't be surprised that one of the main ways you can help others is **with your time.**

Time might be the *best* thing you have to give.

In another letter written by Paul, he says,

Don't forget to do good. Don't forget to share with others. God is pleased with those kinds of offerings.

Hebrews 13:16

Right now, you probably don't have a lot of control over how you spend your time. You have school. You have practice. You have church. You have homework. You can't drive, you can't get a job, and you can't volunteer in certain places until you're older.

So how are *you* supposed to help others with your time? Here are some ideas . . .

- **Instead of watching TV tonight . . .**

- **Instead of playing outside after church next week, help your teacher or small group leader clean up.**
- **Instead of goofing off with your friends after practice, pick up the trash your teammates left behind.**
- **Instead of zoning out and playing video games, search online with a trusted adult for ways you *can* serve in your community.**
- **Instead of hitting snooze in the mornings before school, get ready and help your parents get out the door on time.**

Sometimes, we can get so busy that we forget to spend time doing something for others. But when we *do* share our time, the Bible says that God is *pleased*. In other words, when you **help others with your time**, God gets pumped! He wants to give you a colossal fist bump. (Which He doesn't, because that would probably hurt. A lot.)

◑ THINK ABOUT *ONE WAY* YOU CAN HELP OTHERS WITH YOUR TIME. MAYBE ASK YOUR PARENTS FOR THEIR ADVICE OR HELP. HOW ARE YOU GOING TO HELP OTHERS WITH YOUR TIME THIS WEEK?

....

....

....

WHATEVER YOU DECIDE, *MAKE IT HAPPEN*. DON'T FORGET TO DO GOOD!

DAY 5

OBEDIENCE
EPHESIANS 6:1-3

Parents.
Grandparents.
Babysitters.
Teachers.
Coaches.
Camp counselors.
Small group leaders.
Hall monitors.
Bus drivers.
Law enforcement.

There are lots of people in our lives who we're supposed to obey. It may even feel like you *never* get to do what you want to do, because you're *always* doing what you're told.

If you were in charge, what would you do? Draw a quick sketch to illustrate what you would change if you were in charge:

You may have never thought about it this way, but being obedient is one of the easiest ways you can help others.

Paul writes about being obedient in a letter he wrote called Ephesians. Here's what he says:

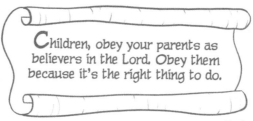

Children, obey your parents as believers in the Lord. Obey them because it's the right thing to do.

Ephesians 6:1

Even though that verse only talks about parents, there are many other places in the Bible that tell us to obey anyone in charge of us. Look a few of them up now:

- **Romans 13:1 is about obeying** ....

- **John 14:23 is about obeying** ....

- **Hebrews 13:17 is about obeying** ....

Being obedient is about way more than respecting people. It's about *helping* people. **You can help others with your obedience.**

Think about it this way . . .

When your mom asks you to pick up your dirty laundry, she's not trying to keep you from playing your favorite video game. She's asking for your *help*.

When your dad asks you to start brushing your teeth and getting ready for bed, he's not trying to stop you from watching your favorite TV show. He's asking for your *help*.

When your teacher asks you not to run in the halls, she's not trying to stop you from having fun with your friends. She's asking for your *help*.

When you think about obedience as being *helpful*, it's a lot easier to be obedient, isn't it?

The next time someone in charge of you asks you to do something, pause before you respond. Remember, **you can help others with your obedience.**

◑ SPEND A FEW MOMENTS PRAYING AND ASKING GOD TO HELP YOU WHEN IT COMES TO OBEDIENCE.

TRY THIS

We would all probably say we want to help others. But as a kid in elementary school, you might think you're too young to help others. Or maybe you think you don't have the money to help others. Or maybe you just don't know any "others" who need help.

This week, I've talked about helping with your . . .

Time
Stuff
Obedience

❷ CHOOSE ONE OF THOSE WAYS TO HELP OTHERS. ON THE CALENDAR ➜ ➜ ➜ SCHEDULE ONE DAY A WEEK FOR THE NEXT FIVE WEEKS THAT YOU CAN HELP OTHERS. BESIDE IT, EITHER WRITE, "TIME," "STUFF," OR "OBEDIENCE." WHEN THAT DAY COMES, TRY TO CONCENTRATE ESPECIALLY HARD ON HELPING OTHERS IN THAT WAY.

You can do it. We are going to be helping you by cheering you on the whole way!

SERVING SCHEDULE

WEEK 1	I'm gonna serve with my:	Day:
WEEK 2	I'm gonna serve with my:	Day:
WEEK 3	I'm gonna serve with my:	Day:
WEEK 4	I'm gonna serve with my:	Day:
WEEK 5	I'm gonna serve with my:	Day:

DAY 1

JERUSALEM COUNCIL
ACTS 15:1-35

What rules do you have at home?

....

....

....

Out of those rules, which one is the hardest for you to follow?

....

Rules are *everywhere, aren't they?*

Have you ever felt like there are *too many* rules? Like no matter how hard you try, you're going to mess up?

Wanna know who else felt this way?

Paul and Barnabas.

Remember these guys? The two friends who were working in Antioch to teach and grow one of the very first churches?

Last week we talked about how lots of people were beginning to believe that Jesus is the Son of God. That's a good thing, right? Well, some people weren't so sure.

There were two sides to the argument:

Old School People = Jews (Jewish Jesus-Followers)
and
New School People = Gentiles (Non-Jewish Jesus-Followers)

To put it simply, the Gentiles were the people who had just started following God. And the Jews had been following God for many years. For these Jews, following God meant following hundreds of rules for their entire lives.

So when the Jews put their faith in Jesus, they kept following the rules they had always followed. But when the New School People, the Gentiles, put their faith in Jesus, they didn't know about all of the rules and they didn't follow them.

That made the Old School People really angry.

Think of it this way: If you behaved well all week long, and your brother got in trouble every day, but you *both* got rewarded with ice cream, that wouldn't seem fair, would it?

That's how the Old School People—the Jews—felt.

So even though both sides believed that Jesus is God's Son, they argued about which rules to follow. Because, well, God had given the Jews a *lot* of rules. About all kinds of things.

Rules like: *'You are not to eat sea creatures such as catfish, shrimp, or octopuses.'* **(Leviticus 11:9-12)**

Here's another one: *'The altar to God should not have steps; otherwise, people might look up the clothes of the person ahead of them.'* **(Exodus 20:26)**

Actually . . . that rule makes a good point.

The list of rules went on and on and on. And while God had good reasons for making all these rules, there were just SO MANY of them. The Gentile Christians hadn't grown up following these rules like the Jewish Christians had, so they probably felt really confused by some of them.

So Paul and Barnabas left Antioch and traveled to Jerusalem to get to the bottom of the argument.

After some discussion, Peter, one of Jesus' friends, stood up to share the decision they had all come to. He explained that God sent Jesus for Jews and for Gentiles. He said, *"We believe we are saved through the grace of our Lord Jesus. The Gentiles are saved in the same way"* (Acts 15:11).

In other words, there is nothing we can do to earn Jesus' love. **The story of Jesus is for everyone**: Jews, Gentiles, American, European, Asian, African, Australian—EVERYONE! —no matter which rules we follow.

DAY 2

TREAT EVERYONE THE SAME
JAMES 2:1-10

Has there been a time when you felt treated unfairly? Maybe . . .

- Someone cut in line in the cafeteria.
- The coach played your teammates more than you.
- Your punishment was worse than your little sister's.

Write about a time you felt treated unfairly:

....

....

....

....

....

....

....

....

In the face below, show us how that made you feel:

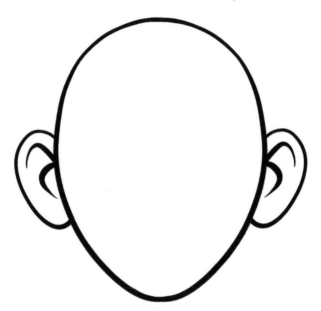

If you drew a frowny face . . . I totally get you. Being treated unfairly is not fun. In fact, it can really *hurt*.

Knowing that, how would you answer this question . . .

Do you treat everyone in your life the same? Think about it.

- **Are there kids at your school who you have trouble being nice to?**
- **Are there players on your team you secretly wish would mess up?**
- **Do you share with your older brother, but not with your younger brother?**

It's not easy to treat everyone the same. But just like it hurts *you* when you're treated unfairly, it hurts others, too.

Jesus wants His story to be for everybody. Jesus wants His love to be for everybody. You know why? Because that's how Jesus loves. And when we know His story, it's easier to love others and treat others the same, too.

James, a friend of Paul's and Jesus' *actual brother*, talked about this in the book of the Bible he wrote called . . . wait for it . . . *James*. Open your Bible or Bible App and read James 2:1-10.

All done? Awesome. Let's continue.

James is writing to Jesus-followers a lot like you. They were tempted to treat people differently, and they didn't always show Jesus' love to others.

But in that very first verse, James says that **if we believe the story of Jesus, we should treat others the same.**

Okay, okay. You can't sit by *everyone* at lunch. You can't invite *everyone* over after school. You're not going to be best friends with *everyone*.

But you can still show kindness to each and every person in your life.
- When the kid who wears the same clothes all the time walks into the classroom, you can smile and say, "Hi."
- When a group of friends comes to your house, you can try hard not to leave anyone out.

- When someone on the other team makes a really great play, you can say . . .

You're not going to get this right all the time—no one does—but it's important for you to *try*.

❷ THINK ABOUT ONE PERSON YOU MIGHT BE TREATING DIFFERENTLY THAN OTHERS. WRITE HIS OR HER NAME IN THE SPACE BELOW.

....

NOW, SPEND A FEW MOMENTS ASKING GOD TO HELP YOU TREAT THAT PERSON THE SAME—TO HELP YOU SHOW HIM OR HER THE SORT OF *KINDNESS* JESUS SHOWS ALL OF US.

DAY 3

GRACE
TITUS 2:11

Fill in the blanks with people's names. Do you know someone who . . .

Has curly hair? ....

Plays an instrument? ....

Is super tall? ....

Is awesome at video games? ....

Has eyes the same color as yours? ....

Is a really good student? ....

God created all of us with different looks, talents, likes, and dislikes. You may have some friends who are similar to you, but no one is exactly the same.

What if I were to tell you . . . we actually *are* the same. All of us. Not in the ways we just talked about, but in a way that matters even more.

After Paul started spreading the good news of Jesus around the world, he wrote a letter to his friend Titus. (Paul wrote a lot of letters, huh?)

Check out how Paul tells us we are all the same because we all need the same thing:

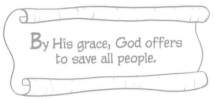

By His grace, God offers to save all people.

Titus 2:11b

Grace. That's a pretty word. You may even know someone named Grace. But *grace* is even more beautiful than it sounds.

Let's try to define *grace* together.

There was kid about your age sitting at the dinner table. His name was Jack, and Jack was not having a good day.

First, Jack forgot his homework. Then, he tripped on the playground and his friends laughed at him. If that weren't bad enough, Jack got in trouble after school for not making his bed.

Jack's mood was three levels worse than bad.

"Can I have another roll?" Jack's sister asked.

"Jack," his dad said, "would you pass your sister a roll?"

But Jack didn't want to pass his sister a roll. Jack's sister made up her bed every single day without being asked. It was probably her fault that he got in trouble.

When Jack didn't move, his sister waved a hand in the air. "Earth to Jack. Are you there, Jack?"

"Jack," his dad repeated. "I said to pass your sister a roll."

Every bad thing that had happened to Jack that day seemed to curl up in a huge ball and get stuck in his throat. He reached for a roll and . . .

"Upstairs," Jack's dad hissed. "Now."

By the time Jack got to his room, his heart was racing. What had he been thinking? His parents were going to be so mad. Jack knew he had done something very wrong.

It wasn't long before Jack's dad came into his room and sat down.

"Jack?" he said. "What do you think your punishment should be?"

Jack couldn't look his dad in the eye. He was so embarrassed. He was so worried.

"No tablet or TV time for two weeks," Jack muttered, knowing he deserved more.

"I agree," Jack's dad said. "But that's not what we're going to do."

"Huh?" Jack asked.

"I want you to come back to dinner," Jack's dad said gently. "Then, I'll take you to get ice cream. It'll be like this never even happened."

That is grace.
Forgiveness we don't deserve.
Love we don't deserve.

And Jesus died so that *everyone* . . .
- **your annoying stepbrother,**
- **the kid who teases you,**
- **that teacher who is always getting on to you**
. . . *everyone* can receive God's grace.

So, yes, we're all different. Each and every one of us is unique. But through grace, **the story of Jesus makes us all the same.** We all are the same because we all need God's grace.

DAY 4

FREE GRACE
EPHESIANS 2:8-9

Have you ever gotten something for free? Something you and your parents didn't have to pay for or earn? What happened?

. . . .

. . . .

. . . .

If you could get *one thing* for free for the rest of your life, what would it be? Draw a picture of it below.

Yesterday, we talked a little bit about the word *grace*. You learned that grace is love and forgiveness that we do not deserve.

Grace sounds pretty awesome, right? We all want grace. But . . . how do we get it?

Can we receive grace by . . .
- **Praying?**
- **Reading our Bible?**
- **Obeying our parents?**
- **Making good grades?**
- **Telling our friends about Jesus?**

While all of those are wise things to do, none of them will get you grace.

So what do you think? What do you think a person's gotta do to get a little grace?

....

....

....

....

....

....

....

Let's see how you did. Listen to what Paul has to say about grace and see how it compares to your answer:

God's grace has saved you because of your faith in Christ. Your salvation doesn't come from anything you do. It is God's gift. It is not based on anything you have done. No one can brag about earning it.

Ephesians 2:8-9

Paul says that you can't *do* anything to receive grace. All you have to do is have *faith* in Jesus. In other words, **because of the story of Jesus, grace is free.**

So, was your answer right? If not, don't sweat it. Grace is hard to understand because it doesn't make sense to human brains.

The best gift ever? For free?! It sounds too good to be true.

But it isn't. When Jesus died, He offered everyone grace. All you have to do is put your faith in Him. Then . . .

Voila! Free grace! Every day. No matter what you do.

❷ IF YOU HAVE TIME, GRAB SOME CRAYONS AND A SHEET OF PAPER. WRITE THE WORD "FREE" IN LARGE, COLORFUL LETTERS. TAPE THE PAPER ON YOUR MIRROR OR SOMEWHERE YOU WILL SEE IT EVERY DAY.

DAY 5

GRACE PASS?
ROMANS 6:15

There are lots of things that require a pass of some sort. Match the pass you need (on the left) in order to do the thing (on the right).

Note from a parent or doctor   Go fishing
Teaching certificate   Drive a car
Fishing permit   Teach school
Driver's license   Arrive late to school
Passport   Travel to a different country

A pass is sort of like *permission*, isn't it? It allows people to do certain things without asking. For example, if you have a note from your doctor, you don't have to ask your teacher if you can stay home from school when you're sick.

If you were in charge, what would you make people get a pass for?

....

....

....

....

Okay! Quiz Time!

Grace is . . .

- ❏ **A gift from God**
- ❏ **Love we don't deserve**
- ❏ **Forgiveness we don't deserve**
- ❏ **Free**
- ❏ **A pass to do whatever you want**

Those all sound pretty true except . . . what about that last one? Did you put a check mark beside it?

If you think about it, you could really take advantage of God's grace. The Bible has already told you that if you put your faith in Jesus, you can get forgiveness over and over and over again.

So, does that mean you stop trying to do what's right? Does that mean you ignore the rest of what God says in the Bible? Does that mean you can do whatever you want? Is grace permission to keep sinning?

Listen to what Paul says in his letter to the Roman church:

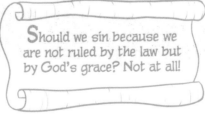

Should we sin because we are not ruled by the law but by God's grace? Not at all!

Romans 6:15

Paul goes on to say that if we use grace as a pass to sin—as permission to do the wrong thing—that means we're ruled by our sin. Paul says it makes *sin* our master.

You have a choice. Is God going to be your master? Or is sin going to be your master? That sounds like an easy decision to us!

When Jesus gave His life, He took the punishment for your sins.

Think about it this way . . .

If your best friend received a consequence every time you messed up, you'd try really, really hard not to mess up, right?

In the same way, what Jesus did for us should make us want to do what is right.

The story of Jesus makes you _want_ to do what is right.

Does that mean you're never going to mess up again? Of course not! But you can try to make wise choices, and you can ask for forgiveness when we fail.

⊙ IN THE SPACE BELOW, WRITE A SHORT LETTER TO JESUS THANKING HIM FOR TAKING THE PUNISHMENT FOR YOUR SINS.

....

....

....

....

....

....

....

....

....

....

....

....

TRY THIS

For today's "Try This", you'll need a pencil and an eraser. You're also going to need crayons, markers, or colored pencils.

I'll hang tight right here while you grab your supplies now.

Oh! You're back. Good. Let's get started!

If you look right over here → → → you'll see the outline of *your* body. Okay. Maybe it's not your *exact* body—but I tried.

Inside that body, try and list any sin you can think of. Here are some words you might use:

selfishness	greed	hate
jealousy	disobedience	dishonesty

When you're finished writing down all the sins you can think of, it's time to erase them. With your eraser, take away all the sins you listed on your body.

Chances are, you can still see traces of the sins you wrote down. But if you put your faith in Jesus, your sins—the things you do that are wrong—are erased from your life as if they never even happened.

That is the miracle of *grace*.

❂ NOW, GRAB SOME CRAYONS, MARKERS, OR COLORED PENCILS. DRAW YOURSELF IN YOUR FAVORITE CLOTHES, UNIFORM, OR OUTFIT.

When God looks at you, He doesn't see your sin. He doesn't even see traces of your sin! Because of what Jesus did, God sees the most perfect, clean, sinless version of you!

DAY I

KING AGRIPPA
ACTS 21:27-36 • 25:23-26:32

Paul lived during one of the most exciting times in history.

You've already learned that Paul worked as hard as he could to tell others about Jesus. But like I said last week, not everyone agreed with what Paul taught. And those who disagreed were *angry* with Paul for spreading the news of Jesus' love. Especially a group of Jews in the city of Jerusalem.

So as Paul made plans to go back to Jerusalem after all of his travels, he was given a very serious warning.

Remember Agabus? The prophet who came to Antioch to tell the church there about the famine? Well, Agabus was back. And this time, God had given him a message for Paul.

Instead of just *telling* Paul what God's message was, Agabus decided to *show* Paul what God's message was.

So Agabus took Paul's belt and tied up his own hands and feet.

Agabus told Paul that returning to Jerusalem would only mean trouble for him. In fact . . . returning to Jerusalem would lead to *Paul's arrest.*

What do you think Paul's reaction was?

....

....

Was this your guess? . . . *Paul went to Jerusalem anyway.* (I bet that wasn't your guess.) And he wasn't there long before the prophecy came true.

A group of angry men found Paul and dragged him into the streets to kill him. His life was saved just in time, but Paul was still arrested and put in jail.

The council in charge of Paul's case didn't know what to do. No one could prove that Paul had broken a law, but no one wanted to make the Jews even MORE angry by releasing Paul.

For his own safety, Paul was moved to a different jail.

There, Paul waited.

Then he waited some more.

Then he waited even more.

Two years passed with Paul in jail.

Go back and reread that last sentence. Can you imagine spending *two years* in jail for no reason? How about two days?

But still, Paul waited.

Then . . . *something finally happened.* An important visitor named King Agrippa was asked advice on what to do with Paul.

When Paul saw King Agrippa, what do you think he did? Do you think he threw himself at the king's feet, begging for mercy? Do you think he pointed the finger at the Jews, claiming his innocence? Not even close.

Huh?!

Why would Paul do that? Why would he waste his opportunity to beg for freedom by telling King Agrippa about Jesus?

Here's why: Getting out of jail wasn't Paul's goal. His goal was spreading the good news about Jesus' love. Paul understood that **the story of Jesus is bigger than any other story**, including his own.

DAY 2

THE GREATEST GIFT
JOHN 3:16

What's the coolest gift you've ever been given? Grab some crayons or colored pencils and draw a picture of it.

Whoa. That's pretty cool. (Okay, I can't actually see it. But after getting to know you, I have a feeling you drew something pretty awesome.)

Gifts are the best thing ever, right? That's why everyone loves Christmas and their birthdays. Imagine either of those days without presents. Would they be as fun?

(It's okay to say no. I love gifts, too!)

There's a verse in the Bible you've probably heard before—**John 3:16**—that talks about *another* gift you've been given.

1. *God so loved the world that he gave his one and only Son.*

2. *Anyone who believes in Him will not die but will have eternal life.*

⊘ TAKE A LOOK AT THAT FIRST SENTENCE. CIRCLE THE NAME *GOD*.

What did *God* do?

He *gave*. UNDERLINE THE WORD *GAVE*.

What did God give?

His one and only Son.

TAKE A LOOK AT THE DRAWING YOU MADE EARLIER. Can you imagine walking up to a stranger and just giving them your favorite gift ever? If so, good for you! You're better than me. In fact, you should probably be writing this book.

God *gave* us His most valuable, most precious, most favorite possession—*His own Son.*

LOOK BACK AT THE FIRST SENTENCE OF THE BIBLE VERSE. DRAW A RECTANGLE AROUND THE SECOND AND THIRD WORDS.

So loved.

Why did God send us His only Son? Because He *so loved* the world. The world = you. **You are part of the story of Jesus. DRAW A LINE THROUGH *THE WORLD* AND WRITE YOUR NAME. READ THE NEW SENTENCE OUT LOUD, USING *YOUR NAME* INSTEAD OF *THE WORLD.***

Jesus came to Earth for one reason—to take the punishment for our sins. When He gave up His life, it wasn't easy on Him. The way He died was very painful, way more painful than anything we've felt.

But He *did* go through with it. Why?

LOOK AT THE SECOND SENTENCE OF THE BIBLE VERSE. DRAW A STAR TO THE LEFT OF "WILL" AND TO THE RIGHT OF "LIFE." WRITE THE WORDS BETWEEN THE STARS YOU DREW HERE:

....

Jesus died so that you could go to Heaven. And how do you get to Heaven? PUT A SET OF PARENTHESES AROUND THE FIRST FIVE WORDS OF SENTENCE TWO.

It's our *faith* in Jesus that gives us eternal life.

God loved *us*.
God gave to *us*.
We believe.
We receive.

You are part of the story of Jesus. In fact, you're a very important part.

DAY 3

HEART EXERCISES
JAMES 4:8

Wherever you are, stand up.

Read through the following list before putting this book down. Try your best to memorize it. *(It's okay if you have to check back.)* Now, do that list! Go on . . . get to moving!

- **25 jumping jacks**
- **25 sit-ups**
- **10 push-ups**
- **Count to 100 while you run in place.**
- **Lie down on the ground, count to 10, and pick the book back up.**

Good job! Did you cheat? I was totally watching!

So, how do you feel?

. . . .

. . . .

. . . .

Now, take two fingers and press them to the side of your neck, right under your jaw.

That *thump, thump, thump* you feel is your *pulse*. You can also feel your pulse at your wrists, inside your elbow, and the top of your foot. *(Which may be kinda stinky right now, so don't check there.)*

Your pulse is your blood pumping through your body. Since your heart is in charge of moving that blood, when your heart beats faster, the blood zips through your veins faster, making your pulse speed up.

This happens every time you exercise. And you already know that exercise is really, really good for your entire body, but it's especially good for your heart.

Did you know there's another kind of heart exercise? A kind that's even *more* important than what you just did?

One of Paul's friends was a guy named James. And James gives us some advice about this kind of exercise. He says:

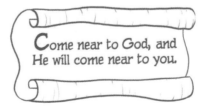

Come near to God, and He will come near to you.

James 4:8a

Come near to God?! How does someone get *near* to God?

By exercising your heart.

Not with jumping jacks and push-ups, but by creating regular habits that make you better on the inside.

Here are a few examples:

- *Praying:* **Talking to God**
- *Reading:* **Reading your Bible, or even a book like the one you're reading now**
- *Worship:* **Turning on some music and singing to God**
- *Serving:* **Volunteering at your church, school, or in your community**
- *Talking:* **Having conversations about God with your family, friends and community**

Don't panic! You don't have to do all of these all the time to exercise your heart. Just choose one or two at a time to focus on.

Each heart exercise draws you nearer to Jesus. He loves this, **because Jesus wants you to know Him and His story.** He'll draw near to you, and that makes life so much better.

❷ THIS WEEK, WHICH OF THESE HEART EXERCISES WOULD YOU LIKE TO MAKE A HABIT? AND HOW?

....

....

....

....

DAY 4

FRUIT OF THE SPIRIT
GALATIANS 5:22-23

You may think that fruits are the most boring snack ever. But check out these crazy fruit facts[1]:

- **A strawberry isn't actually a berry, but a banana and a pineapple are.**
- **Grapes** *explode* **when put in the microwave. (Please DO NOT test out this fact!)**
- **Apples, peaches, and raspberries are all members of the** *rose* **family.**
- **Bananas are slightly radioactive.**
- **The watermelons grown in Japan are** *square.*
- **The world's most popular fruit is the . . . drumroll, please! . . .** *tomato!*

Okay, so maybe you'd still rather eat a bag of chips or some cookies, but fruits *are* pretty cool.

In a letter written by Paul (Yes, he wrote *another* letter!) called Galatians, he talks about a different kind of fruit. Open your Bible or Bible App and read Galatians 5:22-23.

Now, before you start checking your armpits for grapes or your nostrils for blackberries, Paul doesn't mean we're going to produce *actual* fruit. He's using fruit as a symbol. Paul is simply saying that if you know Jesus, people should be able to see some of Jesus in your life.

Think of it this way.

If you walked up to an apple tree and picked a perfectly ripe apple, you would expect to bite into it and taste yummy, fresh apple. But what if you bit into it and tasted something bitter, old, and yucky?

That would be totally confusing!

The same is true when you say you know Jesus, but don't act anything like Jesus. When what you say on the outside doesn't match who you are on the inside, it's really, really confusing to people. **The story of Jesus changes you.** It makes you want to be more like Jesus in how you treat others and in how you treat yourself.

The word "fruit" really means something more like *characteristic*. In other words, the "fruit" describes *who you are*.

Let's take a quick look at the characteristics Paul talked about. He said that if we know Jesus, we will show:

- ❏ **Love**
- ❏ **Joy**
- ❏ **Peace**
- ❏ **Patience**
- ❏ **Kindness**
- ❏ **Goodness**
- ❏ **Faithfulness**
- ❏ **Gentleness**
- ❏ **Self-Control**

❍ MAKE A CHECKMARK BESIDE THE CHARACTERISTICS THAT ARE EASY FOR YOU TO SHOW. CHOOSE YOUR TOP THREE.

NOW, PUT AN X BESIDE THE CHARACTERISTICS THAT ARE SOMETIMES HARD FOR YOU TO SHOW. CHOOSE AT LEAST TWO.

Before you start feeling bad about yourself, don't worry. No one shows all these characteristics all the time. In fact, we need God's help to have any of these characteristics. It's okay to pray and ask God to show you how you can be more patient, kind, or joyful.

LOOK AT THE TWO CHARACTERISTICS THAT YOU PUT AN X BESIDE. WRITE THEM IN THE SPACE PROVIDED, AND THEN WRITE THREE WAYS YOU CAN GET BETTER AT THEM.

> *HINT: We already told you one way just above!*
> *There's also an example on the next page → → →*

Characteristic: Self-control

How I can get better:
3.   Asking for God's help.
4.   Asking my mom to hide the junk food so I don't eat so much that I get a tummy ache.
5.   Taking a deep breath before yelling at my little sister.

Now it's your turn:

Characteristic:

....

How I can get better:

1.
....

....
2.
....

....
3.
....

....

When you put your faith in Jesus, you are in His family. You will be more like Him, because **the story of Jesus changes you.**

DAY 5

BE PREPARED
I PETER 3:15

What are some things you have to *get prepared* for? *(Prepared is just another word for "ready.")* Have you ever prepared for a . . .

- ❏ **Big test**
- ❏ **Piano recital**
- ❏ **Gymnastics meet**
- ❏ **Science Fair**
- ❏ **Presentation at school**
- ❏ **Soccer match**
- ❏ **Chess tournament**
- ❏ **Play at the community theater**
- ❏ **Solo at church**

When you prepare for something, you practice for it. You rehearse. You go over what you're going to do, say and, sometimes even what you're going to wear!

In *1 Peter 3:15*, another one of Paul's friends tells us something very important that we should *all* be preparing for. Check it out.

> **B**ut make sure that in your hearts you honor Christ as Lord. Always be ready to give an answer to anyone who asks you about the hope you have. Be ready to give the reason for it. But do it gently and with respect.

❯ UNDERLINE THAT SECOND SENTENCE—THE ONE THAT STARTS WITH, "ALWAYS BE READY . . ."

Peter is talking about people who have put their "hope" in Jesus. In other words, anyone who has faith that Jesus is God's Son.

WRITE THE FIRST THREE WORDS OF THAT SECOND SENTENCE BELOW:

....

Peter says we should *always be ready* to talk about *our faith*.

Have you ever thought about what you would say if someone asked you who Jesus is? Have you ever thought about what you would say if someone asked you why you believe in Him? Or how you started believing in Him?

It's important that you are prepared to answer them. Since you may be the only way someone hears the story of Jesus, **you need to know the story of Jesus.**

Just like you'd get ready for a spelling test at school, or just like you'd attend practices to get ready for your soccer matches, you should be practicing what you're going to say when someone asks you about your faith . . . and how you're going to say it. Which, according to Peter, should be with *gentleness* and *respect*.

Have no idea where to start? No worries, friend. I've got your back.

(Actually . . . you have my back . . . literally, you're holding my back. But that's not really what I meant . . .)

● THE "TRY THIS" SECTION FOR THIS WEEK WILL HELP YOU COME UP WITH WHAT YOU CAN SAY WHEN SOMEONE ASKS YOU ABOUT THE STORY OF JESUS.

TRY THIS

Jot down your answers to the following questions. You can look back to Day 2 of this week for some help. Don't worry if you're not exactly sure how to put into words what you think or feel. Just try your best.

1. Who sent Jesus to us?

....

2. Why did God do that?

....

....

3. What's the *coolest* miracle Jesus performed? If you don't know of any, look up a few now. *(Some examples are: Matthew 4:24, John 2:1-11, Luke 5:1-11, Mark 6:30-44, Matthew 14:22-23)*

....

....

4. What did Jesus do for us?

....

....

5. When you first started learning about Jesus, what did you think about Him?

....

....

6. Why did you decide to ask Jesus into your heart? What did you do?

AMeLia ....

Katterine ....

7. What are three things you've learned about Jesus since starting this book?

....

....

....

8. What are three words you'd use to describe Jesus?

....

....

....

❂ GOOD. NOW THAT YOU'VE GOT YOUR ANSWERS, YOU'RE SET TO *ALWAYS BE READY*. BELOW IS A SAMPLE SCRIPT THAT YOU CAN WRITE FOR YOURSELF. FILL IN THE BLANKS WITH THE ANSWERS YOU JUST GAVE.

Friend: "Do you believe in Jesus?"

You: "Yeah, I do. Let me tell you about Him. His story is the best story ever told.

The first thing you should know is that **#1** .... sent Jesus to us. He did that because **#2** ....

Jesus was born a lot like us, only cooler, because He was born in a place with animals and hay and stuff. Not that His parents were animals. Forget the animal part. It's not important.

Anyway, Jesus grew up and started teaching that He is God's Son. He did all kinds of cool miracles that proved He was right. My favorite was when He **#3** ....

But not everybody liked Jesus. Actually, some people hated Him because they thought He was lying about being God's Son. So they had Jesus **#4** ....

But three days later, God raised Jesus from the dead!

I know, pretty cool, right? All those things had to happen because God wants to be close to us. But since He's perfect and we're not, we can't be close to God on our own. But when Jesus died, He took the punishment for every wrong thing we'll ever do. He traded His perfect life for our not-perfect life. Because of Jesus, we can be close to God!

But that's not even the best part. When we decide to believe that Jesus is God's Son, that's called having *faith*. And if you have faith in Jesus, you get to live in Heaven with Him one day.

Don't worry if you're not sure what to think about all this. I mean, when I first started learning about Jesus, **#5** ....
....
....

But then one day, I decided **#6a** ....
....
....

So I **#6b** ....
....
....

Since then, I've learned **#7** ....
....
....

Jesus is so **#8** ....
....

But most of all, He loves us no matter what. And He loves you, too.

If you want to come to church with me next week, we should let our parents talk! You'd love knowing more about Jesus."

● YOU CAN *(AND PROBABLY SHOULD)* REWRITE THIS ENTIRE SCRIPT IN YOUR OWN WORDS. MAKE IT YOUR OWN. THEN, LOOK OVER IT FROM TIME TO TIME. PRACTICE. PREPARE. *ALWAYS BE READY!*

DAY I

FORGIVENESS
EPHESIANS 4:31-32

Imagine this . . .

You're Paul.

(Okay girls, this might be kind of weird, but give it a try.)

You're Paul.

You were born in an awesome city. You go to one of the best schools where you're smarter than most of your friends. You grow up and become a powerful scholar and leader. No one messes with you. No one *dares* to get in your way.

Your job is to stop the movement of Jesus-followers by hunting them down and putting them in prison. And you're very, very good at your job.

Then one day, you're traveling with your buddies to arrest more Jesus-followers. Suddenly, a bright light shines down from the sky. A loud voice starts speaking to you, but you can't see who it is. In fact, you can't see anything, because *you're blind.*

And you stay blind for three days before some dude you've never met comes to you. *Ananias* is his name, and when he's finished praying for you, you can finally *see* again.

Everything has become clear to you, now. And not just your vision. You realize that you've believed the wrong thing your entire life. You realize that Jesus IS God's Son!

Then, when you look in the mirror . . .

. . . *you're* the one being hunted for becoming a Jesus-follower. You have to escape from the town that you had once marched proudly toward by slipping through a hole in the city wall.

Back in Jerusalem, you try to make friends with the people who follow Jesus. But that doesn't go so well, either . . .

When they finally *do* believe you've honestly changed, *another* group of people decides they want to kill you. You have to run for your life *again*.

You spend years on the road, telling people about Jesus. And when you finally come back to Jerusalem, you're almost murdered by the same people who would have welcomed you back *before* you believed in Jesus. You barely escape with your life, only to be thrown in jail . . . *for two years.*

Before becoming a Christian, Paul was basically *famous*. Minus those annoying Christians, Paul's life was good and exciting.

But after putting his faith in Jesus? Paul was blinded, chased out of towns, rejected, beaten, almost murdered (more than once), and stuck in prison for no reason.

If I were Paul, I would have been tempted to give up. I might have even walked away from the whole "Jesus" thing and gone back to the easier way of life.

But that's not what Paul did.

In fact, Paul did the opposite of give up.

Paul spent a lot of time in a lot of different jails. But he never stopped talking about Jesus. Even when Paul was held under arrest, he wrote letter after letter, teaching and encouraging others.

Check out what Paul writes in one of those letters:

Get rid of all hard feelings, anger and rage. Stop all fighting and lying. Don't have anything to do with any kind of hatred. Be kind and tender to one another. Forgive one another, just as God forgave you because of what Christ has done.

Ephesians 4:31-32

In other words, Paul said, "Forgive people, because God has forgiven you."

Instead of fighting, Paul said, "Forgive."

Instead of having hard feelings, Paul said, "Forgive."

Instead of wanting to get even, Paul said:

FORGIVE!!

Because Jesus has forgiven us all for so much.

The story of Jesus changed how Paul forgave others. And the same should be true for you. **Because the story of Jesus changes how you forgive.**

DAY 2

FORGIVENESS FOR YOU
PSALMS 103:10-12

Before you get all comfy and cozy, hop up and grab a sheet of white paper.

(Hmm . . . you were probably already comfy and cozy, huh?)

The paper can be lined notebook paper, computer paper, or construction paper—it doesn't matter.

Oh, and while you're at it, grab a pencil and an eraser. (Should I have mentioned that sooner? Sorry about that. I promise I'm getting to the point.)

Right . . .

about . . .

now.

❂ DRAW A BIG HEART IN THE MIDDLE OF YOUR PAPER. It doesn't have to be perfect. You're the only person who is going to see this.

Now, think back on your day today. If it's before lunchtime for you, try to think about yesterday. INSIDE YOUR HEART, DRAW A LARGE, DARK CIRCLE FOR EVERY TIME THAT YOU:

- got angry.
- didn't want to wait on something or someone.
- talked back to your parent or teacher.
- didn't want to share.
- didn't try your hardest.
- disobeyed.
- didn't tell the truth, or the *whole* truth.
- wanted something that you didn't have.
- raised your voice.
- wanted more than what you got.

If we were all being honest, we'd probably have at least 4 or 5 large, dark circles on our hearts. So go ahead and add at least that many.

When we sin, it creates darkness in our hearts. Darkness that's a lot like those large, dark circles you just drew. Those are symbols of our *sin*.

Sin is kind of like a bad cold. It makes our hearts sick. No one likes to be sick.

But we also know that *everyone* sins. So how can we give our hearts the medicine they need to be healthy?

In the book of Psalms, the Bible tells us exactly how we can make these dark circles disappear. Open your Bible or your Bible App to Psalm 103:10-12 and check out what it says.

If someone borrowed your favorite toy—say your soccer ball, or your doll, or your LEGO® set—you would expect to get your favorite toy back.

But this verse shows us how *different* God is. When we give God "evil," or sin, He doesn't give us that same thing back. So, what does God give us?

TAKE AN ERASER AND TRY ERASING ALL THE LARGE, DARK CIRCLES YOU DREW IN YOUR HEART.

Your eraser probably wasn't strong enough to remove *all* the dark circles, but let's pretend it did.

When you give God evil—or sin—He gives you *forgiveness*. And not forgiveness like we can give, but total, complete, absolute, 100% forgiveness. That's why God sent Jesus. Jesus took the punishment for our sin and gives us clean hearts in return.

The story of Jesus is about forgiveness for you.

❂   TAPE UP THE HEART YOU DREW IN A PLACE WHERE YOU WILL SEE IT ALL WEEK. WHEN YOU SEE YOUR ERASER MARKS, REMEMBER THAT BECAUSE OF JESUS, YOUR HEART CAN BE PERFECTLY CLEAN AND WITHOUT SIN.

DAY 3

FORGIVENESS FOR OTHERS
COLOSSIANS 3:13

Have you ever gotten in an argument with a friend? If so, what happened? If not, write about what a friend could do to make you angry.

mean DAD

It's not a sin to get mad at someone. In fact, there's a story in the Bible where Jesus got really, really angry.

> Extra credit: Read about the time Jesus got angry.
> It's recorded in Matthew 21:12-13.

But there's a difference between *getting angry* and *staying angry*.

When you *stay angry* with someone, you don't forgive them. The Bible tells us that *staying angry* is a sin. Check out what Paul wrote:

> Put up with one another. Forgive one another if you are holding something against someone. Forgive, just as the Lord forgave you.

Colossians 3:13

Underline that last sentence. Read it out loud: *Forgive, just as the Lord forgave you.*

That's why we should always forgive others—because God forgives us over and over and over again.

Think about it this way:

Imagine you and your friend have been walking around in a dry, hot desert for days and days. You're both so thirsty that you'd do anything for a glass of water—even slurp it from a dog's bowl.

Now imagine that you can see a humongous water fountain in the distance. You look at each other for one half of a second before you both start *sprinting* through the sand to the water fountain.

Because you're super-fast and awesome, you get to the water fountain first. The moment that cool liquid hits your throat, you almost faint because you're so happy and so relieved.

After you've had your fill of water, what would you do? Let your friend drink, too, right?

But imagine for a moment that you *don't*. You block your friend from moving around you to the fountain. You won't let them by. They never get to drink the water.

That's what it's like when we don't forgive people. We're not being fair, because we want Jesus' forgiveness just like we would want that water. And our friends want our forgiveness just like they would want that water.

When we think about what Jesus has done for us, it helps us see that everyone sins—everyone messes up. That's why **knowing the story of Jesus helps us to forgive others.**

This is true for our friends, our parents, our teachers. It's true for anyone we want to *stay* angry with.

Over the next two days, we're going to keep talking about why it's so important to forgive. Right now, think about someone you're angry with. It could be a sibling, teammate, friend or parent.

◐ WRITE DOWN THE REASON YOU'RE *STAYING* ANGRY WITH THEM. WHAT DO YOU THINK THEY OWE YOU?

VIOLet

....

....

....

NOW, DRAW AN X OVER EACH WORD YOU WROTE DOWN. SPEND A FEW MOMENTS ASKING GOD TO HELP YOU GIVE THIS PERSON FORGIVENESS.

DAY 4

FORGIVENESS FREES YOU
I CORINTHIANS 13:5B

Do you like mazes?

Do you hate mazes?

Either way, give the one below a try.

start

So. How's the maze going? Frustrated yet?

Yep. You guessed it. You're not getting out of that maze, are you? Sorry about that. I just wanted you to understand something about forgiveness.

See, getting trapped in that maze is exactly what it's like when you choose not to forgive someone. It traps you. It makes you feel stuck.

Put a check next to one of the following:

- ❏ **Loving others is important.**
- ❏ **Loving others is not important.**

Paul wrote a letter—(I know . . . he probably wrote more letters than all of us combined.)—to a church in Corinth that talks about love. And if loving others is important to you, this is something Paul says you must do:

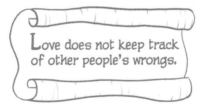

Love does not keep track of other people's wrongs.

1 Corinthians 13:5b

If you know the story of Jesus, you know that loving others is one of *the* most important things Jesus asks us to do. And if you want to love others, you can't keep track of the things others have done to make you sad, mad, or upset.

When you keep talking about or thinking about what other people did to hurt you, it's a lot like locking yourself inside a maze that you can never escape. It doesn't help you. It doesn't make your life better. In fact, not forgiving others hurts you.

But when you do choose to forgive, it's like taking a shortcut to the end of the maze. **Forgiveness frees you.**

Forgiveness *doesn't mean* . . .

- **that what the other person did was okay.**
- **that you have to be friends with someone who hurts you.**
- **that your hurt doesn't matter.**
- **that you can't be sad because someone treated you unfairly.**

Forgiveness means that you choose to not be angry anymore.

If you need to forgive someone and you don't know how, skip to the "Try This" section at the end of this week.

IN THE SPACE PROVIDED, CREATE YOUR OWN MAZE WITH A VERY CLEAR ESCAPE. IN THE TITLE SECTION, PUT THE NAME OF THE PERSON YOU NEED TO FORGIVE. IF YOU CAN'T THINK OF ANYONE, PUT YOUR OWN NAME. SOMETIMES, THE HARDEST PERSON TO FORGIVE IS *YOU* WHEN YOU MESS UP.

title: ....

start

DAY 5

FORGIVENESS FREES OTHERS
2 CORINTHIANS 2:5-8

Have you ever had a pet? If so, which pet has been your favorite? If not, what kind of pet would you like to have?

Sketch a picture below and write that pet's name on the collar.

When you have a pet, it feels like they're part of your family. You'd never think about opening your front door and setting that pet free (not unless you wanted your mom to ground you for the rest of your life).

But being set free can actually be a *good* thing.

We've been talking about forgiveness for the last few days. When we forgive others, it doesn't mean what they did was okay. It just means that we *set the other person free*.

Think about it this way.

When you choose not to forgive someone, it's like taking a set of handcuffs and locking one cuff on your hand and the other cuff on their hand.

Here's what *un*forgiveness feels like:

- **You often think about what they did to hurt you.**
- **You don't speak to them, or barely speak to them.**
- **You say mean things about them to others.**

Even though you may not *like* that person, your unforgiveness keeps them tied to you.

Open your Bible or Bible App to 2 Corinthians. Read chapter 2, verses 5-8. Write down what verse 7 says below:

....

....

....

Paul tells us exactly what to do when we feel handcuffed to someone because we're still mad at them. He says to:

- **Forgive**
- **Comfort**

Paul says we do this so the person we're angry with won't be . . .

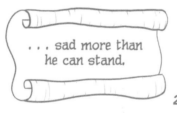

. . . sad more than he can stand.

2 Corinthians 2:7b

We forgive others because **forgiveness frees others.** And, like we already said, we have to forgive others if we want to be forgiven.

You may have heard a song before that tells you to *let it go . . . let it go . . . let it go.*

Is it stuck in your head now? (Sorry!) If you know it, go ahead and belt it out.

That's exactly what Paul tells us to do: Let go of your anger and show kindness to the person who hurt you.

So, how do you do that?

◑ WRITE WHAT HAPPENED AND HOW IT MADE YOU FEEL ON A PIECE OF PAPER. SHOW YOU WON'T KEEP A RECORD OF THE WRONG BY DOING ONE OF THE FOLLOWING THINGS WITH THAT PAPER:

- **Soak it in water for a few minutes and then squeeze it into a tiny ball.**
- **Bury it in the backyard.**
- **Cut the paper into tiny shreds and throw them in the trashcan.**

When you set others free with your forgiveness, you show that your faith is big. You show that you believe that Jesus forgives you for your sins. And because of that, you show others forgiveness, too.

TRY THIS

One of the best ways to end an argument is to apologize for anything *you* did wrong *first*.

Yeah, I know. This doesn't feel easy. And sometimes, it's hard to know what to say and how to say it. But I'm gonna help you!

◑ IF THERE'S SOMEONE YOU NEED TO SAY YOU'RE SORRY TO, ANSWER THE QUESTIONS BELOW:

Who is someone that I need to apologize to?

....

What am I apologizing for?
- ❏ **What I did**
- ❏ **What I said**
- ❏ **How I said it**
- ❏ **Disobedience**
- ❏ **My anger**
- ❏ **Something else:** ....

How do you think it made the other person feel?

....

What's one way you could do better next time?

....

◑ NOW THAT YOU'VE THOUGHT ABOUT WHAT YOU WANT TO SAY, USE THE GUIDE BELOW TO WRITE OUT YOUR APOLOGY ON ANOTHER SHEET OF PAPER AND SEND IT TO THE PERSON WHO NEEDS TO HEAR IT.

Dear .... ,

I am very sorry that I...

....

I know it was wrong because ....

You probably felt .... , and I am very sorry.

Next time, I'll do my best to ....

Please forgive me.

Love,

....

....

DAY 1

PAUL SHIPWRECKED
ACTS 27:1 • 28:10

Paul's life has been pretty entertaining, hasn't it?

He's been the bad guy. He's been the good guy. He's been in danger. He's been attacked. He's been snuck out of cities. He's even been thrown in jail without ever committing a crime. That's more action-packed than a superhero movie!

But what happened to Paul next tops *all of that*.

The last time we saw Paul, he was in jail. One day, it was decided that Paul would travel across the Mediterranean Sea to the city of Rome to stand trial . . . and the best way for Paul to get to Rome was by ship.

Early into the journey, Paul knew that the trip wasn't going to be an easy one. The wind began to blow. The waves got bigger and bigger and bigger. Before long, the ship was struggling to stay on-course.

To make things even worse, the trip was taking way longer than planned and winter was quickly approaching. For the next few weeks, the weather report was nothing but storm after storm.

What do you think Paul did? Did he . . .

. . . **hitch a ride to the nearest island on the back of a dolphin?**
. . . **steal all the life-jackets and throw himself overboard?**
. . . **lock himself in a closet and pretend all the rocking and swaying meant he was on a rollercoaster?**

No, Paul did none of those things (even though I probably would). As we are learning, Paul never took the easy way out. Instead, Paul spoke up.

Guys! If we keep sailing, we're all going to die!

Do you think anyone listened to Paul? *Nope.*

As the ship got back into deep waters, the wind started to blow again. And this wasn't wind like a gentle breeze on the beach. It wasn't even wind like the cold gusts of winter storms. These winds blew so hard that they lost control of the ship.

They started throwing stuff overboard so the boat could stay afloat. They had nothing to eat, and they couldn't see the sun or stars for days.

But the storm still wasn't over.

Thunder, lightning, wind, and waves raged on. The storm continued so long that everyone on the ship lost hope of ever being saved.

But then an angel gave Paul some amazing news.

Looking at the weather, the ship, and the few supplies they had left, Paul had no reason to believe this angel. But he did—**because the story of Jesus changed the way Paul saw his problems.** (And also, when an angel shows up, you listen.)

After two weeks in the storm, they finally made it to an island. The people there cared for them until another ship came to their rescue.

Think about this . . .

When was the last time you thought you had a bad day? Paul's bad days are making our bad days seem . . . not so bad, huh? If we learn anything from Paul's story, we learn that our problems may not be as hopeless as they feel.

(And also, we learn that our lives are really, really boring!)

The story of Jesus changes the way we see our problems, too.

DAY 2

HOPE
ROMANS 8:38-39

Have you ever had to do something that seemed *impossible?*

Maybe you had to . . .

- clean your bedroom after totally trashing it.
- get a good grade on a test that you didn't study for.
- ride your scooter down a really steep hill.
- make friends at a new school.
- learn how to do push-ups in P.E.

In the moment, those things felt *impossible.* But you were probably able to do them, right?

There are some things, though, that really are *impossible.* For example, you could never . . .

- pull a huge tree from the ground with your bare hands.
- jump off your roof and fly (*please do not* test this one out).
- ride your scooter across the country.
- benchpress 1,000 pounds.
- beat a pro-basketball player in a game of one-on-one.
- be separated from God's love.

Did you catch that last one? It is *impossible* for you to be without God's love.

Paul tells us so in the book of Romans. Listen to what he says:

> I am absolutely sure that not even death or life can separate us from God's love. Not even ... the present or the future, or any powers can separate us. Not even the highest places or the lowest, or anything else in all creation can separate us. Nothing at all can ever separate us from God's love. That's because of what Christ Jesus our Lord has done.

Romans 8:38-39

Have you ever had something really sad happen to you? Something that was hard or hurtful? Maybe . . .

- **your parents got divorced.**
- **your pet died.**
- **your dad lost his job.**
- **your grandma got sick.**
- **you broke your arm.**
- **you best friend moved away.**
- **you had to start a new school.**

What happened?

....

How did you feel?

....

How do you think God felt about what happened?

....

❍ LOOK BACK AT OUR BIBLE VERSES AND UNDERLINE THE LAST SENTENCE. WRITE IT HERE:

That's because ....

....

Because of what Jesus did for you, you can always *know* that God loves you. **And because you know the story of Jesus, you can have hope when bad things happen.**

When does God love you? All the time. No matter what. FILL IN THE BLANKS BELOW WITH THE PHRASE, "GOD STILL LOVES ME."

When I feel alone, ...

When I am angry, ...

When I am not good at something, ...

....

When I feel left out, ...

When I mess up, ...

When I am sad, ...

When bad things happen, ...

When you're going through a hard time, remember that it's impossible to be separated from God's love. He is with you, even when it doesn't feel like it.

DAY 3

NEVER ALONE
PSALM 139:5-10

Find a lamp in your house and turn it on.

If this lamp is in your parents' room and they are sleeping . . .

RUN FOR YOUR LIFE!!!

Being *very* careful not to touch anything that's hot, take your hand and put it near the lamp. Now, look on the wall closest to the lamp. What do you see?

A shadow, right? Sketch what your shadow looks like below:

Now, make the following shadow puppets with your hands . . .

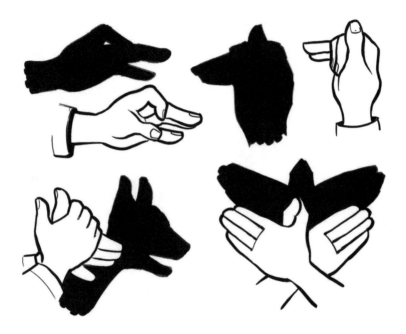

Maybe you've been outside before and you saw your shadow on the ground. Wherever you go, your shadow goes. If you hop, it hops. If you run, it runs. If you cough, your shadow coughs. Your shadow is with you *all the time.*

God is a lot like your shadow. Even when you don't think He's there, God is always with you.

Open your Bible or Bible App to the book of Psalms. (It's right in the middle!) Psalms was written by a couple of different people, and Paul was *not* one of them. But, Paul *did* read it.

When Paul was a kid like you, his parents sent him to a special school where he would have studied all the books in the Old Testament, including the book of Psalms.

The person who wrote the chapter we're reading is a man named David. Maybe you've heard of him. He was the kid who fought a giant named Goliath and then grew up to be the king of Israel.

Now, look up chapter 139 and scan down to verses 5-10. Read what David says to God.

Wow! David was a pretty good writer, huh? And from his writing, we're reminded that God is *always* with us. David says that God . . .

- **is around you.**
- **is behind you.**
- **is in front of you.**
- **goes with you *anywhere*.**

Remember what we learned about Adam and Eve? We learned that when sin entered the world, we became separated from God. Because God is so perfect, He can't be near sin. But then Jesus came! Jesus took the punishment for that sin, and He offers us new, clean hearts. Because of what Jesus did, God can be close to us again!

Because of the story of Jesus, you are never alone.

◑ WHAT'S THE FARTHEST YOU'VE EVER BEEN FROM HOME? SKETCH A PICTURE OF YOURSELF AT THAT PLACE. PUT A BIG STAR BESIDE YOUR DRAWING AS A REMINDER THAT YOU ARE NEVER ALONE.

DAY 4

THANKFUL
I THESSALONIANS 5:18

Write down five things you wish you could buy:

1.
....
2.
....
3.
....
4.
....
5.
....

Now, write down five things that you're thankful for:

1.
....
2.
....
3.
....
4.
....
5.
....

Which list was easier for you to make? If your answer is the first list, you're definitely not alone.

It's easier to focus on what we *don't* have than it is to be thankful for what we *do* have. But thinking this way creates two big problems:

- **Thinking about what you *don't* have only makes you unhappy.**
- **God wants you to be thankful for what you *do* have.**

In his letter called 1 Thessalonians, Paul writes this:

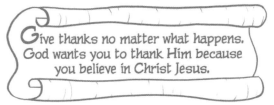

*G*ive thanks no matter what happens. God wants you to thank Him because you believe in Christ Jesus.

1 Thessalonians 5:18

Fill in the blanks with what the verse tells you to do:

Give thanks ....

God wants you to thank him because you ....

....

Paul tells us that **the story of Jesus makes us thankful.**

When Jesus gave His life for you, He gave you the most incredible, amazing, awesome gift that anyone could ever give. He erased all of your sins and gave you a new, clean heart. If you never received one more gift for the rest of your life, you should still *give thanks* for what Jesus has given you.

Which would you rather do? Stand in front of a store window and look at toys you can never buy? Or stand in your bedroom and play with all the things you already have?

Duh! It's way more fun to *enjoy* than it is to *want*. Which is why it's important to teach your mind to focus on what you already have.

There are a few things you can do to practice being grateful.

- **Give – Save – Spend**
  When you get money as a gift or earn money babysitting, give some, save some, and *then* spend some.

- **Get One – Give One**
  Every time you receive a new toy or game, give a used one away to a charity or thrift store.

- **Thank You Notes**
  Get in the habit of writing down your thankfulness. When someone does something nice for you, write them a thank you note. It doesn't have to be on a fancy card, and it doesn't have to be long.

◑ WHEN WE REALIZE WHAT JESUS DID FOR US, IT SHOULD MAKE US SO, SO THANKFUL. WHY DON'T YOU WRITE *HIM* A QUICK THANK YOU NOTE RIGHT NOW?

....

....

....

....

DAY 5

PEACE
PHILIPPIANS 4:6-7

Grab some crayons or markers and decorate the symbol below:

That looks groovy, baby!

Have you ever seen that symbol before? Maybe on someone's necklace, shirt, or on a sign somewhere?

It stands for *peace*, right?

In your own words, define *peace*.

....

....

....

Simply put, *peace* is when your heart and mind feel calm.

What makes you feel *peaceful*? Check any that are true for you:

- ❏ Warm showers or baths
- ❏ A cool breeze
- ❏ A good book
- ❏ Having your back rubbed or scratched
- ❏ Your mom holding your hand
- ❏ Going for a long walk
- ❏ Your favorite blanket
- ❏ Other ....

But there are times in your life when it's hard to feel peaceful.
Like . . .

- During a thunderstorm
- Right before a big test
- In the middle of the night
- When you get in trouble
- When someone you love gets sick
- When your parents argue
- When it's your turn to bat during a game
- Other ....

In the book of Philippians, Paul talks about what we should do during times like those. He says:

> Don't worry about anything. No matter what happens, tell God about everything. Ask and pray, and give thanks to him. Then God's peace will watch over your hearts and your minds. He will do this because you belong to Christ Jesus. God's peace can never be completely understood.

Philippians 4:6-7

When your heart feels sick with worry or stress, Paul says the best medicine is to *tell God everything* and to *be thankful*.

Talking to God + Being Thankful = God's Peace

The next time you start to feel worried, stressed or afraid, tell God. Tell Him exactly why you're worried. Then, tell Him you're thankful because He is always with you.

Now, this isn't *magic*. You might have to pray the same prayer a few times before the worry really starts to change. But over time, if you stick to it, your heart and mind will begin to calm down.

◐ IS THERE ANYTHING YOU FEEL WORRIED ABOUT RIGHT NOW? ARE YOU STRESSED ABOUT SOMETHING? OR AFRAID? IN THE SPACE BELOW, *TELL GOD EVERYTHING.* AND DON'T FORGET TO ADD HOW THANKFUL YOU ARE THAT HE IS WITH YOU, AND HOW THANKFUL YOU ARE FOR HIS PROMISE TO GIVE YOU PEACE.

....

....

....

....

....

....

....

....

....

....

TRY THIS

On Day 4, we talked about gratitude. One of the easiest ways to practice gratitude is to tell others thank you. And I don't mean a quick, "Thanks, Mom!" as you're running out the door to catch the school bus. I mean learning to *really* say thank you—and mean it.

On the next page ➜ ➜ ➜ is a guide to writing (and designing) the raddest, most ridiculously cool Thank You notes on planet Earth.

You're going to need:
- Pen or pencil
- Markers or crayons
- Piece of paper
- Someplace quiet to work

But first! **Who are you going to thank?** Your mom? Teacher? Small group leader? Friend? Super cool aunt? Write their name here.

....

Step One: Fold your paper in half to make a card.

Step Two: Decorate the front by using colors, pictures, or words that remind you of the person you're making the Thank You note for.

Step Three: Copy this paragraph down on the inside of the card, filling in the blanks using the number key below.

Hey ....(1)................. ,

I just wanted to say ....(2)................ for

.................(3)................. .

My favorite thing about you is ....(4)................. .

I am thankful for you!

.................(5).................

1. Name of person you're thanking
2. Choose from—thank you, thanks, thanks a ton,
    thanks a million, muchas gracias
3. Something specific this person did for you: made
    your lunch, helped your math scores, took you to
    the movies
4. A compliment
5. Your name

> *EXTRA CREDIT:*
> *Make 2 more Thank You notes tonight!*

Now, the most important part of writing a Thank You note is . . .

SENDING THE THANK YOU NOTE!

➋ SO, GET TO IT. ASK YOUR PARENTS TO HELP YOU MAIL
YOUR THANK YOU NOTE WITHIN THE NEXT 24 HOURS!

DAY 1

ONE BODY
EPHESIANS 4:4-16

Over the last few weeks, we've studied the lives of two men: Paul and Jesus. For a lot of us, it's hard to think about Paul—and especially Jesus—as being *real* people. But they were. Paul and Jesus really lived.

They ate dinner.
They had a favorite color.
They had bad hair days.
They were *real*.

And when we look at the story of *their lives*, we learn things that help *our* lives.

In fact, check out this cool illustration Paul wrote to explain exactly how our lives fit into the story of Jesus:

There is one body and one Spirit. ... There is one Lord, one faith and one baptism. There is one God and Father of all. He is over everything. ... So we will grow up in every way to become the body of Christ. Christ is the head of the body. He makes the whole body grow and build itself up in love. Under the control of Christ, each part of the body does its work. It supports the other parts. In that way, the body is joined and held together.

Ephesians 4:4-5, 15-16

But before you get lost in the images of heads without bodies and detached arms floating around the world . . . let's think a little about what Paul is trying to say.

There is *one* God.
There is *one* Jesus.
Everyone who believes Jesus is God's
Son is part of *one* big family.
And God is the head of that family.

But just like a real family, we all have roles to play.

Think of it this way.

Maybe you are an incredible listener. Your friends tell you things because you don't talk when they're talking. You care about what they have to say. God made you to listen well. Your role in the body is to be the *ears*.

Maybe you see things that others don't. When someone is sad, you notice. When someone feels left out, you notice. You pay attention to what's happening around you. God made you to *see* things. Your role in the body is to be the *eyes*.

Or maybe you are good at talking in front of groups of people. You encourage people with your words. You are the *mouth* of the body.

If you love breaking a sweat to help others, you are the *hands*.

It sounds strange, right? *I'm an ear? Or an eyeball?* But when you discover who God created you to be, you can play your role in God's big family.

And when we all play our roles, we're like one HUGE body of believers working together to love God and love others. Isn't that cool? **Knowing the story of Jesus changes the way we work together.**

DAY 2

YOUR PURPOSE
PHILIPPIANS 2:13

If the story of your life were made into a movie, what would that movie be called?

....

Which actors would you choose to play the roles of your friends and family?

....

....

What's a scene from your life that would be good *comedy*? (*Example: that time you dressed up like an alien and spooked your mom.*)

....

....

What's a scene from your life that would be good *drama*? (*Example: that time you and your best friend got in a fight over the last slice of pizza.*)

....

....

What's a scene from your life that would be good *action*?
(Example: that time you learned how to do a cartwheel using only one hand.)

....

....

You may not know it, but the story of your life is way, way more important than any movie. **Your story has huge *purpose*.**

Do you know what that means?

It means that your story matters. Your story is *important*. And not only are you important to your friends and family, but you're important to God, too.

Paul talks about this in ***Philippians 2:13***. He says:

God is working in you.
He wants your plans and your
acts to fulfill His good purpose.

Did you know that God is *using* you? He is. He needs you. God needs you to *fulfill His good purpose*.

What do you think the good purpose of God is? Well, that's going to be a little different for everyone. God will use your unique gifts and talents in a different way than He uses your friends' unique gifts and talents.

What are you really good at? What do people compliment you on? What comes easily for you that doesn't always come easily to others?

....

....

....

....

....

....

Whatever your answer is, God wants you to use *that* to spread His love everywhere you go.

As you get older, God's good purpose for you will become more and more clear. All you need to worry about right now is that you keep getting to know Him better.

❍ MOST MOVIES HAVE POSTERS THAT ADVERTISE THEIR RELEASE. GRAB SOME COLORED PENCILS OR MARKERS AND A SHEET OF PAPER, AND CREATE A POSTER FOR THE MOVIE ABOUT YOUR LIFE. TO GET IDEAS, ASK YOUR PARENTS TO HELP YOU DO AN ONLINE SEARCH TO SEE WHAT YOUR FAVORITE MOVIE'S POSTER LOOKS LIKE. OR, JUST USE YOUR IMAGINATION. REMEMBER TO INCLUDE:

❏ **Title**
❏ **Actors' names**
❏ **Release date**
❏ **Colorful image that represents you**
❏ **One sentence why people should see the movie**

❍ HANG THE POSTER SOMEWHERE IN YOUR ROOM WHERE YOU WILL SEE IT EVERY DAY. USE IT AS A REMINDER THAT *YOU* HAVE A STORY OF YOUR OWN—ONE THAT GOD WANTS TO USE TO FULFILL HIS GOOD PURPOSE.

DAY 3

SET AN EXAMPLE
I TIMOTHY 4:12

Check out some of these cool inventors[1]:

- **Abbey Fleck was 8-years-old when she invented *Makin' Bacon*, a plastic dish that hangs bacon from its bars while they cook. Now it's being sold at Target, Walmart, and Kmart!**
- **Richie Stachowski was 11 when a family trip to Hawaii inspired him to invent the *Water Talkie*, which allows people to talk to each other under water. He sold his idea to Toys "R" Us!**
- **Cassidy Goldstein was 12 when she got tired of her crayons breaking and decided to invent *Crayon Holders*, plastic containers that make it easy to hold broken crayons. In 2006, Cassidy was named Youth Inventor of the Year.**

The inventor of the trampoline was 16.
The inventor of earmuffs was 15.
The inventor of the popsicle was only 11-years-old.

If you could invent something, what would it be?

....

....

....

Sketch a drawing of how you picture your invention and give it a name.

Those kid inventors did some pretty amazing things, didn't they? Do you want to know the difference between those kids and you?

Nothing.

Not one thing.

Okay, maybe your name isn't Abbey. And maybe you'd invent something way cooler than earmuffs—like ice cream that doesn't melt or a backpack that helps you fly.

But the truth is, *all* kids can do great things.

Check out what Paul says about being young in 1 Timothy:

Don't let anyone look down on you because you are young. Set an example for the believers in what you say and in how you live. Also set an example in how you love and in what you believe. Show the believers how to be pure.

1 Timothy 4:12

Paul says that being young doesn't mean you don't matter. Young people—kids like you—can be an example to others.

You may think that you have to be a certain age before people look up to you, but that's not true. Your story is happening *right now*. **Your story can set an example for others**—even adults!

Paul gives us a few ways we can set an example:
- **What you say.**
- **How you live.**
- **How you love.**
- **What you believe.**

If you want to be a kid whose story sets an example for others,

Think about what you're saying. Do you show respect to your teachers? To your parents? To your friends' parents? Do you speak kindly to your siblings? Do you blow up and say mean things when you're angry or upset?

Think about how you're living. Are you practicing gratitude? Are you obedient to your parents? Do you always try your hardest?

Think about how you love. Are you willing to share your favorite toys or games? Do you help your parents by doing chores around the house? Do you cheer for other people to do well?

Think about what you believe. Are you talking to God most days? Are you reading your Bible most days? Are you going to small group and listening respectfully?

You don't have to do *all* these things to set an example. No one's *that* perfect *all the time*. Start by choosing one category and focusing on it for a few weeks. Then, switch to focusing on another one.

Which category do you want to choose for this week?
- ❏ **What you say.**
- ❏ **How you live.**
- ❏ **How you love.**
- ❏ **What you believe.**

➊ WRITE DOWN TWO WAYS YOU CAN SET AN EXAMPLE FOR OTHER BELIEVERS USING *JUST* THE CATEGORY YOU CHOSE:

1.
....
2.
....

God wants your story to set an example for others, so spend a few moments asking Him to help you do that.

DAY 4

BETTER TOGETHER
ROMANS 15:5-6

Draw a line matching the movie titles to the character names:

Anna & Elsa	*The Fox and the Hound*
Mike & Sulley	*Alice in Wonderland*
Marlin & Dory	*The Jungle Book*
Carl & Russell	*Monsters, Inc.*
Copper & Todd	*Finding Nemo*
Mowgli & Baloo	*The Lion King*
Timon & Pumbaa	*Toy Story*
Woody & Buzz Lightyear	*Frozen*
Lightning McQueen & Mater	*Cars*
Tweedle Dee & Tweedle Dum	*Up*

Which of these movies was your favorite? If you haven't seen any of these, what is your favorite movie or TV show?

....

The reason we enjoy movies like these so much is that they're all about *friends* doing things together. They're about . . .

- **friends going on adventures together.**
- **friends facing fears together.**
- **friends competing against each other.**
- **friends helping each other.**
- **friends arguing with each other.**
- **friends growing up with each other.**

If we were to watch these same movies with only *one* of those characters, it just wouldn't be as good.

This is true in movies, and it's true in our own lives.

Think about your most favorite memories. Are there any that *don't* involve other people? Maybe a few, but not many. That's because **our stories are better together.**

Grab your Bible or Bible App and look up these verses on working together:
- *3 John 8*
- *Proverbs 27:17*
- *Ecclesiastes 4:9*

These verses tell us:
- **We should help other Jesus-followers spread the truth.**
- **Being around other people makes us better.**
- **We can get way more done together than we can alone.**

Our stories are better together.

Read what Paul said in the book of Romans:

Our God is a God who strengthens and encourages you. May He give you the same attitude toward one another that Christ Jesus had. Then you can give glory to God with one mind and voice.

Romans 15:5-6a

Paul says we should have the same attitude with each other that Jesus had with us. So we should be . . .

. . . **patient.**
. . . **forgiving.**
. . . **generous.**
. . . **loving.**
. . . **kind.**

When we treat others the way Jesus treated us, the Bible says that we can *give glory to God with one mind and one voice.*

What does that mean? Think about it this way . . .

Imagine one person singing on a stage without a microphone.

Now imagine 100 people singing on that same stage without a microphone.

Which would be *louder?*

Which would be more *powerful?*

The choir.

If we learn to work together with others (by treating them like Jesus treats us), we can be like a humongous choir of Jesus-followers, way louder and way more powerful than if we were all alone.

❂ SPEND A FEW MINUTES WRITING ABOUT SOMETHING YOU DID ALONE THAT WOULD HAVE BEEN *WAY* BETTER IF YOU HAD DONE IT WITH A FRIEND.

....

....

....

❂ SPEND A FEW MOMENTS ASKING GOD TO HELP YOU WORK TOGETHER WITH OTHERS. IS THERE SOMEONE YOU AREN'T TREATING THE SAME WAY JESUS TREATS YOU? WHO IS IT, AND HOW COULD YOU DO A BETTER JOB OF WORKING WITH THAT PERSON?

....

....

DAY 5

SHARE JESUS
ACTS 20:24

What are some things that you love to share?

....

What are some things that you do not love to share?

....

Sharing isn't always easy, is it? But it's important—especially if you're sharing something that could really help someone.

Think about this . . .

You and your friend are swimming in a pool together. You're lounging in the shallow end on a float, and they are swimming laps in the deep end.

All the sudden, your friend gets a major leg cramp. They start splashing everywhere and can't keep their head above water.

The only thing that can save your friend is the float that you're sitting on. **What would you do?**

....

You may have put down a silly response, but all of us would throw our friend the float.

Over the last nine weeks, you've learned a lot about the story of Jesus.

(You probably don't even realize how much you know.)

But . . . did you know the story of Jesus is a lot like that float from the example you just read?

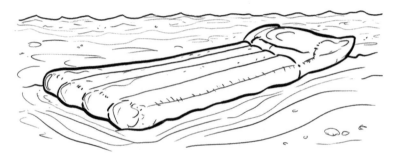

Our world needs the story of Jesus *even more* than the friend needed the float. And now that you know it, **the story of Jesus is yours to share.**

Open your Bible or Bible App and read Acts 20:24. Write the last sentence down below:

He wants me to ....

....

....

....

....

God wants you to share the story of Jesus.

You can:

1. **Invite your friends to church or church events.**
2. **When a friend is going through a hard time, tell them how talking to God has helped you.**
3. **Wear your VBS or church camp shirt to school.**
4. **Treat others with love and kindness. They will notice that there's something different and special about you, and they will ask what it is.**
5. **Give someone a copy of this book. (But not *your* copy!)**
6. **Simply *tell* someone the story of Jesus.**

In verse 24, Paul says that his life "meant nothing" to him. He doesn't mean that his life wasn't valuable. Paul is just saying that nothing he wants or needs is more important than doing what God wants him to do, which is sharing the story of Jesus.

God wants sharing the story of Jesus to be *that* important to you.

❧ CAN YOU THINK OF ONE PERSON YOU CAN SHARE THE STORY OF JESUS WITH NEXT WEEK? REMEMBER, YOU ALREADY HAVE THE GUIDE YOU WROTE FROM THE "TRY THIS" SECTION OF WEEK 7. IF YOU'RE NOT READY TO TALK ABOUT YOUR FAITH YET, THAT'S OKAY. CHOOSE ONE OF THE OTHER WAYS (1 – 5) FROM THE LIST ABOVE.

Using your words or your actions, who can you share the story of Jesus with?

....

How are you going to share it?

....

....

....

When are you going to share it?

....

....

When you share the story of Jesus with a friend, it stretches and grows your faith. Not only that, but sharing the story of Jesus is like throwing someone a float when they're having trouble swimming. It will save their life, and they will always be grateful you were brave enough to share.

TRY THIS

Well, friends. *(Sniff, sniff.)* You've made it to the final section of this devotional journal. *(Long wail.)* Wow. *(Snort, sniff.)* I've had an awesome time hanging out with you. *(Sniff.)* We've laughed, we've cried . . .

(Wait . . . I'm not the only one crying, am I?!)

Out of everything you learned over the last nine weeks, what was (feel free to flip back through the pages) . . .

The most surprising?

....

The hardest to understand?

....

The silliest?

....

The saddest?

....

The most important?

....

◑ LOOK BACK TO THE "TRY THIS" SECTION OF WEEK 1. YOU WERE ASKED TO MARK A CHART TO SHOW WHERE YOU WERE IN YOUR FAITH.

DRAW A NEW MARK ON THAT CHART AND WRITE DOWN TODAY'S DATE.

In the coming days, months and years, you will go through good times and you will go through bad times. But the thing that will *never* change is the story of Jesus. It . . .

changes how you see Him.
changes everything.
changes how you see others.
changes how you help others.
is for everybody.
is bigger than every other story.
changes how you forgive others.
changes how you see your problems.
changes how we work together.

Hang on to this book. When you feel sad, alone, frustrated, betrayed, ignored, worthless or even if you just miss me (*sniff, sniff*), get it back out. Remind yourself of the story of Jesus.

Remind yourself . . .

He loves you forever.
He forgives you forever.

The story of Jesus never changes.